MW00910946

Hobbstown

The Forgotten Legacy of a Unique African-American Community

Cindy Williams Newsome

PublishAmerica
Baltimore

© 2004 by Cindy Williams Newsome.
All rights reserved. No part of this book may be reproduced, stored in a retrieval system or transmitted in any form or by any means without the prior written permission of the publishers, except by a reviewer who may quote brief passages in a review to be printed in a newspaper, magazine or journal.

First printing

This literary work is based on true incidents. Some names have been changed at the author's discretion, and any likeness of those names that have been changed to any living or deceased individual is purely coincidental.

The creation of a 30-year Martin Luther King Youth Center celebration is fictitious and is merely used as the vehicle to historically move the story forward.

ISBN: 1-4137-8041-5
PUBLISHED BY PUBLISHAMERICA, LLLP
www.publishamerica.com
Baltimore

Printed in the United States of America

*When forgiveness becomes a state-of-mind,
reconciliation is always on the horizon.*

Acknowledgments

First and foremost I thank God for commissioning me to write a portion of Hobbstown's history. I am forever humbled. However, the work would not have been possible without oral history from descendants and natives of Hobbstown. Please accept my sincerest thanks for rendering me interviews. To my husband, Willie, thank you for always believing in me. I love you with my whole heart. Thank you Ivy and Mary Nell for being my family editors, and thank you Miranda for always "keeping it real" when I needed it. A special thanks to Richard Nelson for providing so much vital documentation; now you know why you held on to those papers for so many years. Thank you to Ian Bryant, Sallie Pickett, and Richard Boyce, for photos of Leslie Murdock, the Passionettes, and the Admirations, respectively. A very special thanks to Naomi Miller Lauria (posthumously) for remembering and providing the Somerville Raiders' anthem. An awesome thank you to the following women for sharing their wisdom and lives with me: Ms. Mattie, Ms. Anna, Ms. Mott, Ms. Vick, Ms. Odessa, Ms. Loudia (posthumously), Ms. Nora (posthumously) for your interviews, which gave me a sense of post-Hobbstown culture in the south, and early Hobbstown culture relative to surrounding communities. You further provided valuable insight of the personalities of the early settlers. I appreciate those who called me when they heard about the book venture, John R. Stewart, Ken Hobbs, Reverend Doris Thomas, and Latricia Bryant, to tell me of information they believed should be included. Many thanks to Patricia Benesh, Author Assist, for aid with story concept. I thank Bishop Donald Hilliard, Jr., and Pastor Bernadette Glover-Williams, of Cathedral International, for spiritual covering and for their spirit of motivation…and so much more in Christ.

If anyone has inadvertently not been recognized, please know that I sincerely thank you. Following is a list of individuals interviewed. God bless.

Ivy Blue
Ian Bryant
Louise Bryant
Wade Bryant (posthumously)
Modestine Bryant
Diane Cunningham
Geraldine Freeman
Constance Hobbs
James Hobbs, Jr.
Victoria Hobbs
Joyce Johnson
Gertrude Jones
Naomi Miller Lauria (posthumously)
Mattie Mahaffey
James Mahaffey
Betty Miller
Marian Miller
Anna Murdock
Cheryl Murdock Ward (posthumously)
Eric Murdock
Lydia Murdock-Williams
Richard Nelson
Miranda Newsome
Loudia Proctor (posthumously)
Sally Proctor
Judy Robinson
Howard Robinson
Geraldine Stapleton for Coach Vaughn Stapleton (posthumously)
Odessa Stackhouse
Chester Williams, Jr.
Mary Nell Williams
Nearo Williams, Jr.
Mary Williams
Nora Williams (posthumously)

Table of Contents

Prologue
Death of a Native Daughter
11

Chapter 1
In the Beginning—The Quest for Safer Ground
25

Chapter 2
Connections
50

Chapter 3
Awakenings
77

Chapter 4
Stewart's Hill
108

Chapter 5
More School Days—The Minstrel
119

Chapter 6
The 287 Scare and High School
141

Chapter 7
The Passionettes—More School Days, and Death
164

Chapter 8
The Martin Luther King Youth Center and the
Somerville Raiders
191

Epilogue
Hobbstown Today
211

Bibliography
215

Prologue

Death of a Native Daughter

It was December 20, 1968. Leslie Murdock pressed a soft kiss to Eric's cheek and planted another on his forehead. She drank in his baby smell and cradled him close before gently handing her son to her mother, Anna. She quickly pulled on her car coat and smoothed her hair with her hands.

"Mommy, I'm gonna walk up to Cosmos to get soda. Holloway's is closed by now."

"Oh, Les, it's cold out there. Why don't you wait until someone comes along with a car and have them take you? You know how I feel about you all walking on North Bridge Street this time of night. There are no streetlights or sidewalks. It's dark walking that road."

For a moment Leslie almost relented. She thought of the dark three-block walk to Cosmopolitan Bar and Grille, and for a fleeting moment, almost took off her coat. But as much as she loved Eric, she longed for a moment of solitude. *Besides*, she thought, *it's just a fifteen-minute walk. I'll be back in half an hour.*

"Mommy, there's no soda in the house. I'll buy a few bottles. You know everyone will want some once they see it. Don't worry, I'll come right back. I promise." She scooted out the door before Anna could say another word.

Leslie relished the harsh winter air. She pulled the hood of

Leslie Murdock

her coat over her head as the cold wind hit her face and brought tears to her eyes. As she walked the familiar stretch of North Bridge Street her mind turned to school. *I'm going to college,* she thought. She walked briskly, pondering her situation. *I'll make Daddy proud.*

It filled her with sadness as she thought of her late father, Andrew Murdock, Jr. He had known his grandson Eric only briefly before succumbing to cancer that October. The cold bit through her bell-bottoms and she quickened her steps against the blustery weather, lost in thought. She had just passed Dead Man's Lane when she heard the sound of a car horn close by.

"Oh, hey, Cindy," she waved to her Hobbstown friend.

"Hey, Les. Where you headed? Jump in. I'll give you a ride. I'm on my way to Woolworth's to finish some last-minute Christmas shopping."

The invitation was tempting as the cold air whipped Leslie's face. However, she concluded she was little more than a block from Cosmos and it felt good to walk. She savored this time to think uninterrupted. "Thanks a lot, but I'm only going to Cosmos. I'll walk the rest of the way."

"Are you sure? It's cold out here, girl."

"Yeah, it is, but I'll be okay. Thanks anyway."

"Okay. I'll see ya later."

"Later."

Leslie continued her walk. She watched the car lights wane and then disappear over the hill past the Cosmopolitan. It dawned on her that traffic was quite heavy. *A lot of people must still be Christmas shopping,* she thought. She moved closer to the heavy bushes and ditches that lined the side of the street. Cars whizzed by. Tires screeched behind her and she found herself floating in air for an eternity. Or perhaps it was seconds. Time ceased. She felt no pain as she landed as light as a feather on the ground. As fluid threatened to cut off her wind pipe, she gasped for breath, laying face-up in what felt like a pool of wetness.

She tried to scream, but her words were gargled as liquid

invaded her throat, nostrils, and ears. Panic crept through her being much like the stream that would not allow her to speak or breathe freely. *Where am I?* She attempted to pull herself up from the total blackness that had swiftly become her world, but her body would not budge. It was then that she understood she was hit by a car.

The ocean of darkness surrounding her engulfed her senses; everything became dreamlike. She heard muted voices, but could not speak. *Why can't they see me?* Suddenly her seventeen-year-old life exploded before her eyes. In a burst of radiant peaceful light she saw images of her mother, father, and all of her eight brothers and sisters. *Eric, my baby.* She imagined his tiny, smiling face. As her soul ascended from her body and took voyage to the heavens she wondered why she felt no pain, for she had always associated death with pain. And as she soared high above, she knew she was dying. *Mommy, take care of my son.*

———

"Girls, come on," Cindy rushed her daughters. "Let's go. It's 4:00. We need to beat the traffic since it will be like gridlock in Bridgewater this evening."

"Okay, Mommy, we're ready," Ivy assured her. Cindy clutched the steering wheel tightly as she thought of what was ahead this evening. Miranda opened the back door of the car. She threw her pocketbook in and jumped in the back seat. Ivy slid into the front passenger seat.

"This should be crazy fun," Miranda laughed. "We're going back to the Martin Luther King Youth Center. I haven't been in the center since I was eleven or twelve. That's about twelve years."

"Well, what do you think about me?" Ivy laughed. "It's been at least twenty years. I think my last year at the center was around 1982. I was twelve."

It was the summer of 2002. As the girls reminisced about their years at the center, Cindy was lost in her own thoughts. She felt anxious, yet excited. As a local historian, she was asked to be the keynote speaker at the celebration of the Martin Luther King Youth Center's 30th anniversary. The windows were down and a warm breeze flowed into the car as they set out for the center. The soft jazz on the radio helped soothe her nerves, and she began to unwind. Soon they approached the exit that would take them to North Bridge Street and Prince Rodgers Avenue, the location of the center. However, North Bridge Street was never quite the same after Leslie Murdock was accidentally hit by a car and died one lonesome night in 1968.

"Mommy, are you okay?" Ivy reached over and placed her hand on her shoulder.

"Oh, I'm fine. It's just that everything has changed so much here since I was a child. The Bazooka Lounge up ahead used to be the Cosmopolitan Bar and Grille back in the day. Cosmos was the only business establishment on North Bridge Street in those days. As teens living in Hobbstown, we walked there for soda and cigarettes because it was close."

"I thought you all went to Ms. Holloway's for stuff like that since her store was right in Hobbstown?" Miranda asked.

"Yes, we did. But Cosmos was open late, and Holloway's only sold soda and candy."

"Yep, Randi. That was before your time. My friends and I used to love going to Holloway's."

They passed Bazooka's.

"Um, this area was nothing but fields at one time, tall trees and bushes as far as you could see. Oh, I almost forgot, there was a large farm too, Vogel's Farm, it was located where we first exited on to North Bridge Street. The library, vocational school, medical center, post office, and the bank came into existence many years after we were grown.

"As a matter of fact, John Stewart, everyone called him Rollin, and his wife Victoria, owned a home back in the '60s where the bank sits today. It was a beautiful split level. As young children we thought of reasons to visit them just to see the house.

Eventually, the bank came along and bought them out. When they sold the property to the bank, the Stewarts moved out of state.

"The Bridgewater shops on Dead Man's Lane also came later. Oh, I meant to say Prince Rodgers Avenue. It actually used to be called Fourth Street. But Hobbstown called it Dead Man's Lane. The Prince Rodgers name evolved sometime in the late 1980s when a 19th century slave cemetery was discovered on Foothill Road. In the cemetery they found tombstones for Prince Rodgers and his wife Dina, her maiden name was Hoagland. History says he was a slave of Christian Van Horn, and when the state passed a bill in 1804, which freed slaves on their 25th birthday, Prince Rodgers was freed in 1839 on his birthday. He is said to be the first freed slave in the area. The couple was Ms. Victoria Hobbs' grandparents, and many of their descendants still live in Hobbstown."

"Where did the name Dead Man's Lane come from?" Ivy asked.

"Yeah, I bet a dead man didn't have anything to do with the name. You know how folktales get all mixed up," Miranda commented.

"Um, but not in this case. Oral history dating back to around the time Amos Hobbs moved here, tells a story of a dead man found in the middle of the lane. At that time there was nothing but undeveloped dirt roads along here. Ditches were everywhere. Supposedly, the man had on a Sunday suit, but was barefoot. Strangely enough, they say it couldn't be determined what race he was. His face was distorted and swollen, and he was bald-headed. From all accounts, he was never identified. So that's how the street came to be unofficially called Dead Man's Lane.

As she passed Prince Rodgers Avenue, she envisioned that long ago, unforgiving ditch. "You know, girls, there were many times that I thought if only Les had gotten in the car with me that night, things would have turned out differently. A room at the center was dedicated to her memory and a painting of her hung on the wall. I used to tease her and tell her she had *white girl legs* because she had big calves. She would laugh and say, 'Girl, you are crazy.'"

"I heard she was really pretty," Miranda commented.

"She was, and her personality made her even more special. She was even-tempered and sweet. But she'll never be forgotten because she lives on in her son Eric. God has really blessed his life.

"The new house is sure a lot different from the Sugar Shack," Cindy continued, as she decided to take Monmouth Avenue and circle back around to the center. They still had some time. "That's what Ms. Anna called the Murdock's early homestead; the white house they lived in for many years. Eric had it torn down and replaced with the gorgeous Tudor you see there after being drafted into the NBA."

"That house is bad," Ivy remarked. "When Eric went pro it was so exciting. I'll never forget that."

"Yes, that was in '91," Miranda said. "I was only thirteen, but I remember how everybody bombarded the Murdock house that night. Cars were lined up all over Hobbstown. There was such a crowd that we couldn't even get in the house to see Eric. Remember that, Ma?"

"Yes. I could never forget that. TKR Cable was there along with other news reporters. Camera crews were all over the yard. That was an awesome time for Eric and his family, as well as Hobbstown. A native son from humble beginnings soared to the top with God-given talent."

Cindy reflected on her talks with Ms. Anna, Eric and, later with Gerri Stapleton, Coach Vaughn Stapleton's wife. She smiled inwardly as she remembered how Ms. Anna told her that she really didn't quite realize the enormity of Eric's talent before he was drafted into the NBA.

"Well, my brothers would say, 'Anna, Eric can really play.' They practiced with him a lot. This was even before he started high school at Bridgewater-West. And I would say, 'Well all the kids can play.' Because you know, all the kids played basketball at the Hobbstown Park. And I just thought whoever got the ball and dunked it in the basket was the good player. But when he got to the high school, Coach Stapleton took a special interest in Eric, and he kept getting better and better at the game. By this time I really understood basketball more fully, that it was teamwork that made winners. But, I still could not grasp the extent of how his life would change when he went pro. He said, 'Ma, start getting the stuff together that you want to keep because I'm having this house torn down.'

"I said, 'Torn down. Eric, I'm trying to fix *Sugar Shack* up.' Well, he explained that he would be playing professional basketball, but I said, 'But where are you going to be working while you're doing that?' I tell you at that time the whole thing was over my head," she said and laughed.

However, as Cindy remembered her talk with Gerri Stapleton, Coach Vaughn Stapleton recognized Eric's potential at the outset. "He came home one evening and confided in me, 'You know, Ger, there's this one kid on the team; I really think he's going to be great. His name is Eric Murdock.'

"Shortly after that, Vaughn began to help Eric select the right classes to get him into a good college. The two became very close, like father and son. Eric and some of his cousins from Hobbstown, Darrow, Michael, Tyson, and later on Jason, worked our seven-acre crop farm behind the Villa Restaurant on route 28. During this time, Vaughn would always advise the kids that getting a good education was the most important thing they could do. Well, Eric got accepted to Providence, where he excelled athletically and academically. Even after Eric was drafted into the NBA, Vaughn's advice to him was always to invest wisely, so when his NBA career ended he would still be financially okay.

"We had some really good laughs when they were at the farm because it was almost always a disaster every time they came out. They broke lawnmowers, they cut through extension cords. I remember Vaughn would say to Tyson, 'Tyson, you're cutting the hedge, watch out for the cord,' and he would run through the cord. And yes, Vaughn did say, 'I don't want to give those kids a handout. I don't think it's right.' So they came out and worked.

"But, oh, Vaughn and I did have such a good time with them. It was funny, because they would come to work on a Saturday morning, and Vaughn would say to me, 'Ger, the kids are going to be hungry, so could you make some breakfast?' Then lunch time it would be the same thing, 'Could you go buy some hoagies or sandwiches?' And the children really enjoyed being around us and we loved having them at the house, especially since we had no children. And today, each of these young men are professionals. I'm extremely proud of them, and I know Vaughn would be so very proud."

The last time Cindy saw Eric at the Murdock home, he had a basketball tucked neatly under his arm. They talked for a few minutes, and she asked him how he felt when he was drafted into the NBA. "Oh man," he said. "It's something that's hard to explain. The feeling was unbelievable, almost like I was having the best dream of my life, except it was for real. I kept waiting for somebody to wake me up.

"But honestly, at the same time, there was some inner wrestling because I didn't want to let the folks down that helped me get to this point. My uncles had coached me along, and my extended family in Hobbstown was really behind me. Coach Stapleton had helped me tremendously. He had become like a father to me, and I loved him deeply."

She smiled as she remembered Eric's response when she asked what his relationship was like with Hobbstown now that he was a celebrity. "Oh, the relationship will never change," he said warmly. "When I come home to Hobbstown, I'm just Eric, the homeboy, and that's just how I like it; to keep it real."

However, Eric's older cousin, Jonathan Williams, the son of

Jerry and Mary Williams, became the first African-American from Hobbstown to become a professional athlete, while Eric became the second. Jonathan was drafted into the National Football League (NFL) in 1985. Today Jonathan resides in Norton, Massachusetts, with his wife and three children.

It was a sweltering hot day when Cindy spoke with Mary at her home, along with her sister Naomi, about that special time in their lives. Sadly, Mr. Jerry Williams died in 1995. Mary, Naomi and Anna Murdock are sisters.

"Well, Jonathan, Nate, Abraham, all my sons played football well, but Jonathan was a natural. At first he was too young to play with the Pop Warner team. And then on one occasion he was there when the older boys were registering for the team. Anyhow, by the time football was to start that year, he would have had a birthday, and would be of age to play. That's how he was able to go ahead and get on the team. He was always in sports starting with Pop Warner. He played football and baseball, those were his sports. And he definitely came along at the right time, when more doors were opening up for blacks. From Somerville High he went on to Penn State on a scholarship for football, and was drafted to the New England Patriots in 1985 as a third-round pick."

"What impact did his being drafted to the pros have on your family?"

"Oh, you couldn't tell 'honey' (Jerry) anything. It was so exciting. We watched the draft on TV, and in the background you could hear the announcer calling out, 'running back,' and calling names and so forth. We stood on pins and needles waiting for Jonathan's name to be called, and then they called it, 'Jonathan Williams!'

"Well, we went wild." She laughed. "It was so special, and hard to express how wonderful it makes you feel as parents…to see such a great accomplishment for one of your children. When Jonathan got hurt some three years after being drafted, it was hard. He loved the game and had been playing professionally for about three years when he got a severe knee injury. He was in a cast for a while. Jonathan felt that if the doctor did not give him a 100 percent okay, then he wasn't comfortable playing. He really missed it because that's what he loved to do. But he did play for quite a few years, and he was happy with that."

As she continued driving, the saying, "The apple doesn't fall far from the tree," dawned on her because Lydia Murdock was aunt to Eric and first cousin to Jonathan. Lydia had experienced regional and international success as a singer in the late '70s and early '80s when she began performing with a local band, "Satisfunction." Among others, the band included Tyrone Stackhouse, the band's founder, and he also hailed from Hobbstown.

Cindy remembered how she and Lydia had such good conversations about the ups and downs of the entertainment world.

"Well, I went in blind-sided as a solo singer sometime later," Lydia said, "I had a manager, but I didn't have an agent, and I knew very little about the entertainment industry. But my demo in New York was accepted and I signed the contract just like that. I was just a hometown girl, and was thrilled to have a record on the radio, but scared to go to New York! And the glamour and glitz, oh, I was captivated with it. I was making what I thought was nice money. Regrettably, I didn't investigate the business end. It was so exciting to be picked up in a limousine and whisked off to the airport to Paris and London for singing engagements. You know, getting the star treatment. I lived out of a suitcase for six months between Paris and London. You have people buying you beautiful outfits, but the costs of those items eventually come from whatever is being paid to the performer."

"I know there was so much that we didn't know either as singers," Cindy agreed. "And for us it was trial and error because in the '60s it was so difficult to get a contract. But you were really on the fast track overseas with your hit, 'Superstar,' everyone was so proud of you too. In terms of Hobbstown, I think you've accomplished more than anyone in the music field."

"Well, I was proud of you guys when you had the singing group. You'll never know how much you all motivated me back in the '60s. My sisters Cheryl and Leslie, and you and your sister Diane had a great 'girl group.' I would hear you all practicing at our house, or maybe singing in the park and I would say, 'That's what I'm going to do when I'm older.'"

And she did do it, Cindy thought proudly as they reached the MLK Center. She parked the car and took a deep breath. *I'm ready. This history must be told for future generations as well as past. It's time to take the podium.*

———————

Eric Murdock/Coach Vaughn Stapleton
1991 Eric Murdock drafted to Utah Jazz

Jonathan Williams

Chapter 1

In the Beginning—
The Quest for Safer Ground

I'm honored to be with you today to celebrate thirty years of the Martin Luther King Youth Center. Although the center is located in Somerset Manor, which is the official name of the community, its unofficial name, Hobbstown, is the name to which it is most widely referred. We cannot celebrate the center without relating the amazing story of the town and our dedicated ancestors who helped build it.

Hobbstown was born in the 1920s of one African-American man's need to better his life and that of his family. Amos Hobbs migrated north with his family from the racial bowels of Georgia. In the south he had seen, if not experienced, every derogatory occurrence known to black folk, black folk who worked from sunup to sundown picking cotton, who, as sharecroppers, were cheated by farmers and who were the victims of beatings and unimaginable cruelties.

Sista fled for her life, holding her enormous stomach to support her unborn baby. The midday Georgia heat scorched her body as she sprinted towards the muddy water of the brook. She had to throw the hunters off her trail.

"Lord, let me make it there befo' they catch me," she prayed out loud. Her sweat-drenched dress stuck to her body as she ran. "If I can jus' make it to the river before they see me I can hold my breath underwater to get away."

As a young child, living close to the river had its advantages because sometimes, after the cotton was picked, her father would allow her to swim the shallow portion of the river. She learned the escape route in the wee hours of the morning when she and her parents fled a lynch mob in Mississippi. She was ten years of age and sleeping on the floor of the one-room shack they called home that early morning when her mother firmly shook her awake.

"Get up, chil'. We got to run." Her mother's words pierced through the pitch-black room, and at the same time, penetrated her heart with unshakable fear. Her mama threw a blanket around her and half-carried, half-dragged her out of the house to where her father waited in the darkness, crouched behind tall bushes next to the river.

"I don't care what happen, ya'll jus' keep close to the water. If you hear anything, breathe in deep as ya can, slip way down in the water and hold ya breath long as you can, and swim with all ya might," her father warned.

Suddenly there was rustling in the bushes, and then the penetrating sound of her mother's death scream as the blast of a shotgun cut through the night, taking her life. Sista was shaking like a leaf as she heard what sounded like a stampede. She could no longer see her father in the darkness, but she heard him call out, "Why you shoot her? You white devil." Her father's words hissed and resounded through the dark woods like an omen for she could hear he was digging his own grave. "I worked for you all them years, and somebody gone tell you I stole something and you believes it?"

"Nigga, who you talkin' to?"

The blast was all she heard. Trembling, she slipped down into the river without taking a breath to heed her father's words. For the next two days she swam underwater by day and walked the shore by night, laden with tears. She cried as she rummaged through garbage and picked cotton across the state, making her way to relatives in Valdosta, Georgia. It was 1908.

Now, ten years later, she was reliving the nightmare. The mob was dead on her heels. She could feel the hot breath of the old white man who accused her of stealing food from his store.

"Grab her," she heard the old man's voice as she dived into the water. She felt her baby kick in rebellion. At the same time, steel-like hands gripped her arm and dragged her to shore. She felt like a trapped animal as the mob surrounded her. Terror rendered her incapable of moving on her own anymore. Sista was trembling like a leaf as she saw the old man's face. It was contorted with hate to the point that she barely recognized him. As the men kicked her and beat her about the head, she fell to the ground with her arms around her stomach, struggling to stay conscious. But something inside her longed to breathe her last breath rather than feel the hands plummeting her body, attempting to rip her apart.

"You black nigga gal. You gone hang for what you done."

Sista felt the world going dark, but even as she was losing consciousness her mother instinct sought to save her unborn child. "I ain't done nothing, suh. Please have mercy on my chil'." Although she strained to continue speaking, she relished the blackness that overcame her. One of the men held her while another placed a rope around her neck. As she fell into blessed blackness the last thing she heard was, "Nigga, you gone hang today."

———

"Amos," General yelled at the top of his lungs as he banged on the door. It was after 2:00 a.m. in the morning but he couldn't go home. Not in the state he was in, not after what he had seen. He hadn't slept a wink on the train ride back to Buena Vista from Valdosta, and had then run the two miles nonstop to his brother's home.

The door opened and General almost fell on Amos in his haste to enter. He felt drops of sweat pouring down his face and he knew he had alarmed his brother because Amos' face was riddled with concern.

"Lord, what's done happened, General? You hollin' loud enough to wake the dead." General gasped for air as Amos led him over to a chair. He didn't take his eyes off Amos as he went to the water bucket in the kitchen, dipped some out into a glass jar, and brought it back to him.

General drank deeply and sat the glass on the table before speaking. "It's bad. 'Bout the worst it could be," he said, putting his head in his hands and just sitting for the longest time. Amos asked shakily, "The family alright?"

"Yeah. Yeah, they all okay. But you best sit down. It's been a lynching."

"Gone way from here. Way at?" Amos asked. General heard the panic in Amos voice. That panic questioned how close, and how much danger were their families in?

"Valdosta. A young girl. I was leaving Valdosta on my way back to Buena Vista after checking out them farming jobs I told you 'bout. I was walkin' the dirt road that led into town, headin' to the train station. As I came round a curve in the road, a old black woman ran up to me, hollin' and cryin'. I tell ya, I could smell trouble, just the way she was carryin' on. My heart like to froze.

"'They gone hang Sista. I know they is,' she said. 'Chased her off from the sto' way they say she stole some bread. Sista ain't stole no bread. She be too scared to do anything 'round whites. Always scared they gone kill her. And she just 'bout to have her baby.

"From where we stood, I could see part of a river and could hear voices low across the road on that side. I knew it was time to take cover in the bushes or somethin', but the thought of a young girl bein' hung stopped me and I couldn't leave. The old lady was crying somethin' awful and I just couldn't go 'way from there with the state she was in.

"'That's way they ran her off to?' I asked, and the woman pointed towards the river.

"I musta' been thinkin' crazy 'cause I started walkin' over there, like what could I do?

"'No, don't go that way,' she said. 'They might can see ya if that be them over there. It's a patch a trees over yonder on the other side that's high up. That way we can look down to the river and be hid.'

"Sho' nuf, as we climbed to the area where the thick trees was, the voices was louder. Lord, Amos, I never felt so helpless in my life. I couldn't do a thing to help her. The girl was layin' on the ground, still. I couldn't tell if she was live or dead. There was 'bout six white men standing over the girl. Then two of 'em lifted her up while another one took a rope and put it round her neck. When they was done, my God, she hung from the tree. I could see her eyes. They was wide open.

"'After this, niggas a be scared to come in these parts,' one man said. 'They mens and womens.' Then this same man pulled out a sharp huntin' knife from his pocket. I couldn't look no' mo' after that. But I could still hear 'em talkin'.

"'Light the fire,' I heard one of 'em say.

"The old woman cried and fell to the ground. We couldn't leave from there right then. It was too dangerous. I was sick and disgusted at the same time 'cause I couldn't do nothing.

"'Come on. Let's get out of here,' one of 'em said.

"I must a sat there under the tree for I don't know how long, wonderin' why we was born. Then when I come to my senses I saw the old lady walkin' down the embankment and I followed her. What I saw just 'bout froze my blood. They set her body on fire, but you could see it went out after it just about burnt her legs up. You could see the dead baby — they had cut her stomach open."

"Jesus," Amos said, "Lord, Lord, Lord," and kept shaking his head back and forth. General shed some much-needed tears while Amos prayed for his brother and for the young girl's family.

—•••—

As Amos set out at daybreak that Monday morning for the huge farm the brothers and many other men and women in the area sharecropped for a living in Buena Vista, he worried about General. It had been two days since he had come to the house and told him about the hanging in Valdosta. When he arrived at the farm he saw his brother, along with some of the other farmers already working, talking low, and looking anxious. It was harvesting season and after picking up his equipment at the shed, Amos joined them.

"How ya'll doin' this mornin'?" he asked, eyeing his brother, who looked gloomy. General just nodded his head as if to say he was alright, but Amos knew his brother. He loved people. Amos knew that because of General's inability to intercede during the lynching in Valdosta, the wind had been knocked out of him. Amos could tell he was feeling low, depressed.

They were in the tomato field, chopping and crating tomatoes. "If this hangin' over in Valdosta don't make Negroes leave from down here, I don't know what will," Alfred Bell said. Amos saw General wince, and begin cutting the tomatoes off their vine with a vengeance, but he did not speak.

"I got my two daughters and wife to worry 'bout," Alfred continued, "and I done made up my mind to leave for Chicago. Got some relatives out there that's gone help us 'til we get settled on our own."

"Sho' nuf?" Amos leaned on his hoe and wiped sweat from his brow. "I been thinkin' on leavin' the south and taking my family up north, too. I'm sick a being cheated on this farm every year. I done hitched up mo' mules than I can count, plowin', plantin' cotton and everything else, but I ain't never been rightly paid for it. Slavery ended in 1865, but every time you turn 'round it's a hangin' and they gettin' closer and closer to home."

30

"You right, Reverend," Bell said. "The Ku Klux Klan havin' a field day, and the onliest way to escape it is to move as far away from the South as possible."

Amos saw Satchell Brown look around to see who was within earshot besides those he wanted to hear, as he gathered tomatoes in a large bucket.

This ought to be good, Amos laughed to himself, *because Satchell sure could talk some foolishness.* A wave of pity came over him as he pondered on Satchell's life. The years of picking cotton on the farms of Mississippi and Georgia had left him with a hunched back and a bad leg that dragged when he walked. Plus, his wife had run off with another man, leaving him to raise their three children. Amos surmised that Satchell hadn't been altogether right since. He was kind of withdrawn, and talked out of his head at times. Amos looked over at General, who, at forty-two, was three years younger than he and the picture of good health. He had his shirt off and his muscular brown physique glistened with sweat. They had all worked hard from the time they were youngsters. He thought about himself, how the years of hard labor had taken a toll on his body. Although he was still lean and youthful, some evenings it was all he could do to make it home and fall into bed from exhaustion. *Still,* he thought, *compared to Satchell, they were in good shape.*

"Say the girl stole," Brown began, "so might be they had reason."

"Brown, is you crazy?" Bell jumped in.

Brown dropped his head. Amos noticed that he was limping worse than usual as he walked off a distance before continuing to speak. "But that freedom fighter, what's her name, Ida Wells. They say she gone bring her crusade through here soon. Say she got a whole bunch a folks that be marchin' wit' her against hangin's."

"Aw, Brown, she might be coming, might be not," Alfred was getting loud now. "I can't wait on that. Not and they killing our women and daughters now. Lord, no, I can't wait on that."

"Ya'll can't go nowhere. What ya gone do for a livin' if'n you leave here? You best be trying to stay 'cause you don't know nothin' but pickin' cotton and thangs. Got to be crazy to leave way from here and don't know how ya gone live up north. Least here our families got food on the table and a place to stay."

Alfred and General both shook their heads and kept on working. But Satchell's words struck a chord within Amos because he was wrestling with the thought that farming was his life's work. He couldn't think of his love of farming without thinking of his parents, Amelia and Amos, Sr. They had been slaves, who passed farming down to Amos and his siblings like a family heirloom. As a result, they were all masters at tilling the earth. He thought of his brothers and sister with fondness, and how close they were; Moses, Stallin, Jimmy, William, Jason, Jefferson, General George Washington, Robert, and Mary Elizabeth.

As his gaze fell on Satchell, he had to admit that he was right in this case, because he was comfortable with sharecropping and he loved farming. But it was barely enough for the survival of his family of a wife and seven children. On the other hand, he believed if any of them stood a chance of making it up north, it was General. His brother had learned the craft of building merely by watching, and helped erect some homes in the area. Amos felt good that he had also picked up the trade, but General was a natural builder. And now it was end of year harvesting and there was a dull ache in his belly because today Mr. Dunleavy, the owner of the farm, would tell them if they had any end-season wages coming.

"Satch, way you goin'?" Amos heard General call to Satchell as he limped away from the field towards the shed. Amos could hear Satchell's familiar hoarse cough, but he didn't respond to General and walked on as if he hadn't heard him. *Somethin's wrong with him,* Amos thought, because Satchell would work from sunup to sundown non-stop, to the point of eating his lunch between rows of vegetables without leaving the field as he was now.

Suddenly, Satchell fell to the ground. Amos grabbed his water jug as everybody in the field ran to see if Satchell was alright. But when Amos looked down at Satchell's still body, he knew he was dead. Bitterness welled up in him in a way that he didn't know he possessed, and he saw himself possibly just like Satchell in a few years. Dead from heat stroke and overwork.

When Mr. Dunleavy rushed to the scene, Amos observed the nonchalant way he treated the death of a man who worked his farm for more than fifteen years.

"What happened to him?" Dunleavy asked, matter-of-factly.

Amos spoke up. "He was pickin' tomatoes; just like the rest of us, and next thing we knew he fell out, probably heat stroke. Lord, Satchell."

Sunstroke in the soaring temperatures was no stranger to the farmers. Amos had witnessed it more times than he cared to remember. From what he had seen, if a person didn't die from it, the quality of life after a heat stroke usually confined the person to the bed.

"Well, he didn't have much left in him anyway," Dunleavy said. "Just a matter of time. I let him stay on here 'cause I felt sorry for him, but he hadn't been pullin' his weight in a long time."

Amos asked God to help him hold his tongue. *Satchell was 'bout the most loyal somebody he had workin' for him, Amos thought. Yes, he was a might slow 'cause of his ailments, but he had gone out of his way to please Dunleavy by working longer hours than any of 'em. And look what that loyalty had done for him. Ol' Satchell was lyin' on the ground; dead from trying to be loyal to a man that now said he was a charity case.*

"I reckon ya'll can gone leave early. 'Bout mostly done anyways," Dunleavy continued. "I'll take care a gettin' in touch with the authorities and next a kin. After ya'll get ya things together, I'll be in the shed to settle up for the year's work."

Amos grabbed up his gardening tools and was the first to

approach Mr. Dunleavy at the shed.

"Well, Hobbs," Dunleavy said, as he spat a wad of tobacco on the ground, "you ain't got nothin' comin' to you 'cause your fertilizer, hoes, and other supplies out-run ya wages. Then too, it wasn't a real good crop year neither. Look here at the papers."

Amos didn't have to look at the papers because he knew he was being cheated again. "You mean I get nothing for the whole year's work, Mr. Dunleavy, suh? I hardly made but a few purchases at the general sto' this year. I saw to it."

"Made more than you thought. Naw, nothin' this year, Hobbs. Maybe things a work out better next year."

Amos was too tired in spirit to argue the point. He had been through this same scenario many times before. He turned quietly and walked away from the man that sank his manhood to a new low every year. On the mile long walk to the bunking quarters that he and his family called home, he prayed out loud to God.

"Lord, Jesus, I can't stay here and keep on being cheated. What should I do Lord? I gotta make things better for my family."

He was less than a block away from home now and could see his wife Frances' silhouette through the thin curtains of the lone window in the house. Suddenly he was hit with a revelation like Saul on the road to Damascus, and the scales fell from his eyes.

"Bell is right, and Satchell just didn't have much choice after 'while with all his ailments," he spoke out loud. "But I got a choice. I'm still healthy. And we got to leave here soon if it's any hope that my kids can have a better life."

Yet the North seemed as distant as the stars shining down on him from the warm night sky. At forty-five years old he was uneasy about the availability of work if he did go north. And he couldn't shake how Frances might feel about leaving her relatives in the South. After all their years together his love for her had grown deeper, if that were possible, and he remembered 1898 when they first met.

"I'm Amos Hobbs. Ain't seen you 'round these parts," he said to her after church service. "You new to the area?"

He could tell she was shy because she dropped her head and her voice was little more than a whisper when she answered. "I'm Anne Frances Hicks. It's nice to meet you. No, I live in Ellaville. I'm just visitin' the church today with some of my folks."

"That ain't far from here," Amos said, thinking about how he could get lost in the beautiful black tresses that fell to her shoulders in waves. He refrained from the temptation to reach out and touch her striking golden face. "How 'bout if I visit you sometime? I mean at your church, if that's alright?" he asked. His heart pounded out of control as he waited for her answer. When she looked up at him, Amos felt himself falling hopelessly in love with this beautiful creature with the misty brown eyes.

"I'm sorry. I have to go," she said.

Amos was momentarily crushed. However, he wasn't one to give up.

"Hope to see you soon," he said. He saw the deep flush of embarrassment move from her neck to her face. She abruptly turned and walked away.

The next Saturday Amos and General got hold of a steam car and drove to Ellaville. It wasn't hard to locate Frances' home since the Hicks family was well known in the town.

"You got to be crazy, Amos. The girl didn't say she wanted to see you again?" General said, as he honored Amos' wish to drive him to her home.

"Yeah, but she didn't say no either. General, I got to see her again. I need to see her 'cause there was somethin' so strong between us when we met."

As they neared the home, he spotted Frances and another girl walking down the street towards the home.

"Stop, General. I just want her to see me." General jammed on the brakes. Amos got out and leaned on the car. He could tell that Frances recognized him; her face flushed.

"How do?" Amos asked. She and the girl spoke and disappeared into the home. His heart raced as a few minutes later Frances came out of the house and peered down the street to where he and General sat in the car. She walked to the vehicle and, if Amos had anything to do with it, into his life forever.

"Will you marry me, Anne Frances Hicks?" he teased.

"Why are you sitting in front of my house?"

God she's pretty, Amos thought. *Even more so now that she was angry or pretending to be*, he thought. "When we met at the church, you didn't say you didn't want to see me," Amos answered.

"I didn't say I did either," she said.

He liked her fire, and laughed quietly to himself. *If she didn't want to see me*, he thought, *she wouldn't have come out of the house*.

Amos cupped her face in one hand so she could look in his eyes. She didn't resist. "You tremblin'," Amos said. "You not afraid of me are you?" he asked. "That's the last thing I want."

"Just afraid of how you make me feel." Frances' voice sounded faint.

Amos was in Ellaville every weekend after that. He was serious after a not-too-lengthy courtship when he popped the question as they walked home from a nearby park. "Marry me, Frances. Will you marry me? I think I loved you since I laid eyes on you."

"And I love you too."

They married at Ebenezer Baptist Church, the church Amos attended in Buena Vista. A few years later he was ordained in the same church as a minister.

"I'm pregnant," Frances whispered in Amos' ear as she leaned over him to place food on the table one evening. Amos jumped up from the table and grabbed Frances in his arms.

"You mean to tell me I'm gone be a papa?"

Frances laughed softly and they held each other for the

longest time. "We gone have plenty babies, Amos, and God's gone provide."

He laughed out loud now as he approached the door because she had not been wrong. When he came through the door, the four youngest of their seven children jumped on him from every direction. He decided to wait until after supper to tell Frances about Satchell and to talk to her about his plans. The kids would be settled down for the evening by then.

"Frances, Satchell dead. He fell out on the farm today. Seem like it was heat stroke."

He saw Frances catch her stomach in shock. "What's gone happen to them children now? Nobody even know where they momma is. Lord, Jesus."

"Well, I reckon some a they other relatives a see 'bout 'em. It's sad though, one minute he was talkin' then the next he was gone way from here. But it really started me thinkin' even more 'bout leavin' from down here. Frances, I'm studyin' 'bout visitin' Robert and Ella in New York."

"Robert still working in construction up there? Ain't nothing wrong is it?"

"Naw, naw, darlin'. Nothin' wrong. What I got a mind to do is go up by myself and see 'bout work and just study how things is up there. See for myself if we ought to make that move. You know that Valdosta killin' really got everybody shook up and I just want ya'll to be safe. Plus, I'm tired a being cheated on that farm. Didn't get a penny today for all my year's work. The way I feel is I can't do no worse then if I stay here, that I know, and I might do better."

Frances sat on the end of the bed and brushed her hair. Amos could tell she was uneasy because she sometimes bit her lip when she was anxious.

"Robert been trying to get you and General up there for a while, so you might as well gone see."

"All you got to do is say you don't want me to go, and I'll just forget about it," he said. But he prayed she wouldn't change her mind.

"Well, to be honest, since that child was murdered over in Valdosta," Frances sighed, "I been scared to death worrying about these kids. Lord knows we need to go somewhere." She laid the brush on the bed and placed her arms around Amos' neck. "Don't worry about me and the kids. You go on up there and see how it is 'cause I'm ready to leave from down here probably as much as you. If we can make it better up there, then we might as well do it now while we still young enough. The kids can help me around the house. We'll be alright."

A few weeks later, Amos left Georgia on a train for Brooklyn, New York. He stayed with Robert while he checked out employment opportunities on the railroad and in construction. It wasn't long before he landed a job in the maintenance department with the Brooklyn Manhattan Transit (BMT) subway in New York City. Amos was anxious to reunite with his family, especially after Frances sent him a letter telling him she was four months pregnant. It wasn't until after he wrote and told her that he found a job that she gave him the news of her pregnancy. At first he was troubled that she hadn't told him this news before he left. However, he understood that she realized that if she had told him, he would have stayed in Georgia.

After finding housing, Amos went back south in early 1919 and brought his family north by train. Frances was big with child by then. She gave birth to their eighth child in late 1919. The family was extremely cramped in the small apartment they rented in the city. City life was a tremendous adjustment for the family. While Amos believed they were in a safer environment, they all missed the look and feel of the South.

In 1920 the family crossed paths with Millie Murphy, a white realtor, who also lived in the city. That Sunday afternoon Amos and his family stopped at the local corner store to purchase penny candy for the children after leaving services at Cornerstone Baptist Church. He immediately noticed the tall, heavy white woman as he entered the store. She spoke loudly to Roger Douglas, the storeowner, and she waved her hands as if she were agitated. As she spoke, she had one hand on her hip and shook her finger at the air with the other.

"I'm telling you, Roger, we're in a rough situation with this land out there in Bridgewater. Those folks are wealthy, and a lot of this land we're trying to sell was passed down through inheritance. They don't want it though; they just want it sold. We've even tried to sell it to white city folks as summer property, but nothing doing."

Amos saw how the lady observed his family as they entered the store. Her eyes were wide, curious. *Perhaps she had never seen a large colored family,* he thought. He hurriedly picked out some candy so they could leave.

"How long has it been on the market, Millie? You got to give it some time," he heard Mr. Douglas tell her.

"Roger, that property has been for sale for three months now and the owners are threatening to go to another realtor if we don't get some buyers soon."

Amos hurried to the counter to pay for the candy. Frances and the children waited for him at the door, lined up like soldiers.

"Excuse me, sir," the woman said to Amos with a smile, "you and your family live here in the city?"

Amos was taken aback. He looked at the hefty white woman briefly and then looked away before he spoke. "Yes, ma'am," he said, picking up his bag after paying Mr. Douglas.

"My name's Millie Murphy," she said. She extended her hand to Amos. He glanced at Frances. She was biting her lip and giving him a look that said "hurry."

"Got some beautiful property out in the country in New Jersey you might be interested in seeing. It's prime real estate at a good price. The lots are small, but large enough to build a nice size home for your family."

The woman beckoned with her hand for Frances to come over. The realtor piqued Amos' curiosity when she talked about the country. She appeared sincere, but Amos remained cautious as he extended his hand and said hello.

"Amos Hobbs is the name, ma'am. This my wife, Frances. I 'preciate ya offer, but we ain't got that kind a money. Been here 'bout a year and still gettin' settled."

"I guarantee you can afford it," she said, and Amos thought to himself that, she was *right pushy.* "The area has good schools for children and is located in a prime area. Why don't you meet me here next Sunday about this time? You and Frances can follow me out to New Jersey to take a look. It's less than an hour drive."

She can talk up a blue streak too, Amos thought, but he could tell by the look in Frances' eyes that she was taken with what the lady said. She often talked about Georgia and how she missed the country air. Frances looked at him now and he knew she was waiting for him to speak. The spark in her eyes ignited his soul, for he had not fully seen that spark since they left Georgia. Amos was thinking hard because the woman was white and appeared to be going out of her way to get them to look at the property. He wondered what kind of shape the land was in. But he loved seeing Frances happy and he thought, *After all, why did we move here if not to better our lives?*

"Well, might be we'll take you up on your offer," he said, laughing softly, almost to himself.

"It's a deal then," Millie said with a bright smile. "I'll meet you here at the store at 3:00 p.m. next Sunday and we'll drive out to Bridgewater."

As the three shook hands, Amos felt a warm glow in his belly, as if something awesome was just on the horizon.

"Why the truck got to be acting likes it's gonna stop now. Any other time, it just goes right on wherever," Frances lamented. It was the following Sunday and Amos' old pick-up truck sputtered along behind Mrs. Murphy's car during the drive to New Jersey.

Amos didn't want to tell Frances the truck had seen its best days and was subject to quit any time. The truth was the truck didn't owe him a thing. He had been putting away a few dollars every week since he landed the job with the transit, saving it up for a rainy day. *Well,* he thought, *the money would either go for a newer truck or for the land, if it was as reasonable as Ms. Murphy said it was.* He had explained to her that they didn't have much money. However, she told them that, after a small down payment, it was possible they could make payments.

"It's gone be alright, just need to warm up some," he tried to comfort Frances. But he breathed a sigh of relief when they arrived at the land site. He helped Frances out of the truck.

She laughed as she breathed in the country air and exclaimed, "Oh, Amos, this is the place. It feels like back home."

Amos could tell she had fallen in love with the area on sight, but he took it slow. He walked around the land as he considered if he could actually do this thing financially. Also, as far as he could perceive, the place was desolate. Although, he did notice there was one small unoccupied house sitting off a dirt road. He didn't know the racial makeup of the area. He assumed other colored folk must be nearby, otherwise he doubted if Mrs. Murphy would be attempting to sell them the property.

It appeared to be a nice country area to rear their eight, soon to be nine, children. He walked a distance from the property and bent down to pick up some of the rich brown earth. It felt cool and moist in his hand, as if it was waiting for him to nurture it to its full potential. *I can get me a mule and farm a piece of this land just like I did in the south. We can grow our own crops.* His mind was racing with ideas. *Get some pigs and chickens too.*

"Amos." Frances startled him as she called his name, and he realized he had walked a distance from the property. He trotted back to where the two women stood. Frances eyes begged the unstated question. He nodded his head in approval and she squealed with delight. Mrs. Murphy hugged Frances, and Amos saw the look of undeniable relief on the realtor's face.

When they arrived back in Brooklyn Amos discussed his plans with Robert.

"I'm gone write General and ask him to come up and help me build the house. You know, I'm gone need yo' help too," he said.

"And I'll help you all I can."

When General's letter came Amos ripped it open and gave it to Frances to read.

Amos,

I'll be comin' up in a few weeks on the train and I'm thinkin' hard 'bout maybe lookin' for work and then sendin' for the family later, like you done. You and Robert start gatherin' all the sheetrock and supplies you can befo' I get there so we can go right to work on the house. I know you want to get in the house soon, 'specially with Frances gettin' ready to have another baby. Well, I sho' look forward to seein' you all in a few weeks.

General

Frances handed the letter back to Amos.

————

"You and Robert gone ahead and sleep in the truck," Amos said on the first night of building. "All of us can't sleep comfortable in the truck."

"Who gone sleep out here with you?" Robert asked.

"Aw, I'll be alright. Ya'll a be right here."

"Naw. It's warm enough that we can all sleep right here on the ground," General reasoned.

Amos looked up at the sky as a shooting star streaked through blackness. It lit up the area where they stood. He took this as a sign of God's approval.

"Well, Frances put plenty blankets in the back of the truck so all of us sho' could sleep out here." This became their permanent sleeping arrangement as they built the home.

"Lord, just let the truck hold up 'til the house get finish," Amos prayed as he, General, and Robert hauled cement, sheet rock, lumber, and whatever was necessary to build the house. The lot was 30 by 75 feet. Amos found it was just enough property for a two-story house with a small amount of yard space in the front and back. They were now two months into building. Amos was tired and mentioned it to General one day. The truck had finally died, but Amos tried to get to the building site every night after knocking off at the New York Transit. Some evenings he walked from the Somerville train station if one of his brothers wasn't available to pick him up. And other times he took a taxi.

"Why don't you just stay on over in Brooklyn durin' the week then come out here on the weekends. Me and Robert can handle the house," General insisted.

"Naw. Even if I'm able to knock just one nail in the house a day, I'm gone be out here every day that I can. Look like at the rate we goin' we may be done in another few months. What you think?" he asked General.

"Should be done in 'bout a month if we keep going like this," his brother said.

————

Amos stopped for a break one month later as they completed the last of the four apartments in the home. As he took a swig of water from his jug, he noticed his brothers hauling a big slab of wet concrete on plywood to the house.

"What's that for?" he asked.

"Thought we ought to let folks know the year the house was put up and who built it, so Robert's gone write our initials in the concrete," General replied. "When it's dry it will be around forever. Whew, it's heavy too. Got to be 'bout a thousand pounds."

Robert picked up a stick and began writing in the wet slab.

"Well, just put ya'll names on it. Ya'll done most of the work," Amos said.

"Naw," Robert replied, "you was out here every day workin'. What you mean?"

"No, but not from sunup to sundown like ya'll. Naw," he insisted, "just put ya'll initials on it and leave mine off."

Amos stood as his brothers looked at him in surprise. Robert wrote, "This is Hobbstown, G.W. & R.B. Hobbs, Builders, September 17, 1921." The three brothers placed the stone upright in the front yard.

Amos moved his family in just in time for Frances to give birth to their ninth child, Mattie. They soon became aware that they were the only Negro family living in Bridgewater Township, although everyone's address was listed as Somerville. Some of the surrounding white communities, Green Knoll, Martinsville, Bradley Gardens, Branchburg, Raritan, and Finderne appeared indifferent to the large black family that settled in to what they thought of as swamp land, the valley, or just a hole in the back. The family learned the majority of Negroes in Somerset County resided in the actual town of Somerville, which was located about two miles from where Amos and his family lived.

———

Robert and Ella moved into one of the apartments in the home. General went south to bring his family up by train. He didn't have any qualms now about leaving the South and told anyone who would listen that his share-cropping days were over.

"Hurry up, Viola," he teased his wife on the day they were to leave, "we not gone miss that train if we have to leave what little bit we got down here." He knew she was just as excited as he was. It was good to see her laugh as she packed a huge basket with all kinds of delectable food for the three-day trip. She crammed it heartily for the six members of their family. General

Hobbs Brothers—Reverend Amos Hobbs, sister, Mary Elizabeth, General Hobbs & Robert Hobbs

pondered on whether they would be making this trip had all eleven of their children survived. It still cut him to the quick as he thought of how one right after another had died from childhood diseases, malaria fever, pneumonia, and polio. But he smiled as he thought of the four children who lived; from the oldest to the youngest, Amanda, Charlie, Loudia, and Nora.

It's alright, he said to himself, but as he glanced at his wife a tinge of worry washed over him. She had taken the death of their last little boy to illness especially hard. For a while she could not be consoled and took to the bed for long periods of time. He had feared she would never come out of her grief. As he thought about it, she had taken that death even worse than the death of Nora's twin brother. *Maybe 'cause Nora was just a baby then and needed her immediate attention*, he reasoned. His heart bounced with joy in that moment that she seemed so happy.

"That's the best thing that could a happened,'" she had said when he told her about moving north after the brothers finished building Amos' house. He could hear her humming now as she finished stuffing the basket with thick ham and cheese sandwiches, fried chicken, cookies, and homemade sweet cakes that some of the family brought them for the trip.

"Just 'bout ready," she said. "General, did you talk to the children 'bout stayin' in the colored car on the train? We don't want no trouble on the way up there. It's gone be hard for 'em to sit still all that time. Three days, Lord!"

"And I pray this a be the last time they ride on a segregated train or bus anywhere," General said. "No more ridin' in the colored car. I'll talk to 'em good on the way up. They'll be alright."

General felt good during the ride to New Jersey as he thought about the future. They stayed in the car that was designated for Negro travelers. The ride was smooth and the kids played games with each other to pass the time away. The train took them all the way to Bound Brook where they rode the trolley to Somerville. Relatives picked them up at the station and took them to Amos' house where General's family settled into the homestead in one of the apartments.

———

Shortly after the families moved into the rural countryside, Green Knoll tax maps began depicting the area as Somerville Manor. However, the large stone the brothers placed in front of the homestead remained intact. As it went, local taxicab drivers cemented the Hobbstown name throughout the area. Since the street names were not apparent, the cabbies would say, "Oh yeah, we know where you're at; out there in Hobbstown."

The Hobbs' were busy settling their families and didn't give much thought to the name of the community. Their homes were not connected to the city sewer utilities at that time, so inside toilets were not possible, nor was running water in the home. They pumped water from abundant wells and heated it on coal stoves for cooking, personal hygiene, washing clothes on scrub boards, and whatever else it was needed for.

As he learned the town of Somerville, Amos met most of the colored folk that lived there. He particularly enjoyed his trek to a Jewish-owned store on Franklin Street in Somerville where they sold collard greens and other goods his family had enjoyed in the south.

It didn't take long for him to hear the wealth of stories that circulated in the local Negro community about a man named Paul Robeson. And whenever Robeson's name was mentioned he noticed the black folk who discussed him swelled with pride.

Like so many other times, James Rose of Somerville fell in step with Amos one day as he strolled into Somerville. Amos was on his way to his favorite store. *Oh, Lord, here come Rose,* Amos thought. *It's a wonder you can get a word in edgewise.* Amos understood that Rose prided himself on his knowledge of Negroes from the area who went on to bigger and better things. Within minutes Amos saw that Rose was in rare form as he gave a blow-by-blow history on Paul Robeson's roots to Somerville.

"No, Rev, the white folks around here hadn't seen the likes of a Negro as smart as Paul Robeson. He made things better for the Negroes coming after him in this area. I know, 'cause my cousin Winston went to Somerville High with him. Shucks, you passed right by the church his Daddy, Reverend Drew Robeson, pastored back in 1910, St. Thomas A.M.E Zion. Reverend Drew was a runaway slave. In 1904, when Robeson was about six years old, Maria, his Momma, burned to death after her clothes caught fire over a coal stove. But even through that tragedy, Robeson had magnificent gifts and spirit, and there was no stopping him."

In the six months or so that Amos had been in the area he already knew that folk joked about how Rose embellished his stories. However, he could tell from James' countenance as he told this story that he was serious. The words tumbled from his mouth as though he himself had walked alongside Robeson.

"So what did Robeson do?" Amos edged in a question. "I heard some other people talkin' 'bout him at the sto', 'bout how he was a star athlete and such."

"Rev, let me tell you, he changed the way white folks viewed coloreds around here, that's for sure. In 1912 he attended school here at Somerville High. It was just a handful of Negroes and maybe two hundred whites. He was a powerhouse of talent. He could sing and act, and he was one of the greatest athletes these parts had ever seen. In 1915 he graduated with honors from Somerville High and won a four-year scholarship to Rutgers College from a statewide writing competition. When he got to Rutgers he was only the third Negro to attend the college. Even though the white teammates didn't want him on the team, he became Rutgers' star athlete and a great scholar. He won fifteen varsity letters in football, baseball, basketball, and track. He's over there now at Columbia University studying law. Got married and started professional acting, too. Yeah, ain't no doubt that he'll continue to be a special man to our race."

"Sound like he made some real strides. And he was right here from Somerville, huh?" Amos asked. "I got 'bout five children in the high school right now."

"Yep, he sure was," Rose beamed with pride. "Don't worry about your kids in school here. They gone do fine. Good teachers and not too much race problems. Yes, sir, seem like when Robeson came through here things started to change for the better."

"Well, seem like we just got talkin' good and here we is at the sto'," Amos remarked.

"Alright, Rev, nice talking to you. Have a good day."

Amos chuckled to himself because he knew Rose was headed back up the street looking for his next casualty of the day. He entered the store and quietly laughed as he thought of how they were being blessed. With each new day he felt more confident that he had made the right choice in moving his family north. However, it would remain to be seen if Paul Robeson's accomplishments carried much weight in Bridgewater. The white folks seemed to tiptoe around them in the months they had been there. They drove through the developing town as if to see if it was true that Negroes were indeed in the valley.

Chapter 2

Connections

After Reverend Hobbs and his brothers settled their families into the homestead, they wanted to share their good fortune, "God's Country," with those left behind. They began engineering the migration from south to north of family and friends who eventually settled in the town. The brothers' camaraderie set the benevolent tone that became the hallmark of the community. Bridgewater was fast becoming one of the wealthiest townships in the state and, prior to the evolution of Hobbstown, was lily-white.

"General."

He stopped what he was doing when he heard Vi call, but before he could get to the front of the house she had bolted up the steps.

"Say, General, where are you?"

He was placing windows in the home at the rear of the house they recently completed for Robert and Ella. It was right across the street from Amos' home. General placed the pane on the ground and hastily ran to the front of the house. *What in the world is going on?* he wondered. He saw Vi on the top stair of the porch. Frances, big with baby number ten, stood on the ground in front of the porch. She leaned on the rail of the portal. General looked at Frances for a sign, but she gingerly sat down on the bottom step and was silent. He watched anxiously as Vi quickly made her way down the stairs. Relief flooded his body because her eyes lit up like the sun, which told him that she was in high spirits. They were luminous now as she looked at him.

"General, I was down there in back of the house gettin' wood and a white man come up to me. He kind a scared me, too, 'cause I didn't see no car a nothin' when all of a sudden I heard a voice right behind me. Seem like he come out of nowhere. He said, 'If you think you might want to buy this property, I'll sell it to you cheap.' Said his name was Mr. Hackendun. And said I should talk to you 'cause he really wants to sell it quick. You know him?"

"Naw, not as I recollect. Hackendun, huh?"

"Yes, that's what he said. Now, what he said, too, is he'll be back through here tomorrow in case we want to talk to him 'bout it. What you think?"

General weighed his words cautiously. He didn't want Vi getting her hopes up only to be let down. Oh, he was making ends meet doing shift work at the Johns-Manville plant in Bound Brook. They used some of Amos' land for farming and things were going well enough, but he was itching to build his own home and disappointed thus far that he had not found a favorable land deal like his brothers. Judging from the look on her face, he could tell Vi was thoroughly convinced that whatever this man had told her, she was sold. *Still*, he thought to himself, *he probably wanting more than I can afford to pay.*

"Vi, let's wait 'til Amos and Robert get off work, then we can all look at the property together. You know how good Robert is at cuttin' them deals. He knows how to talk 'em down on they price."

"General, the man said $500 dollars for three-and-a-half acres. Said he can work it out so we can make payments of $15 dollars a month. I don't think we gone find a deal better than that."

"Aw, Vi, I don't know." But his heart leaped at the possibility.

51

"That's a right smart amount of money every month. Let me see what Amos and Robert think."

"Seem like to me since we gone be payin' for it, we can sho' nuf decide between me and you if we can buy it."

He saw Frances look away as if she hadn't heard Vi. She then hoisted herself up from the stoop. "I'm going on back to the house so I can start supper."

"Alright. Let's gone in the back and look at the land," General said. He was already surmising he would have to get some extra building jobs to come up with the hefty mortgage payment. *$15.00 dollars a month. That's a lot of money,* he thought.

In early 1923 General moved his family into the home he built on the three and a half acres he purchased from Mr. Hackendun. There was plenty of land for crops, and after a while he quit his job at Johns-Manville since he didn't care for the shift work. He went into business for himself building houses and farming. After a while, he bought a pick-up truck and started another business, corrugating boxes from the white folks in town.

Meanwhile, Amos had kept in touch with his friends from Cornerstone Baptist Church, Hill and Cora Miller. He stopped by their apartment after knocking off work at the Transit one evening.

"Ya'll come on out to the country for dinner this weekend," Amos said to Hill and Cora as they sat in their living room. "They still got a right smart amount of land for sale out there. Ya'll ought to think about buyin'. It a give you chance to get out of the city and feel more like back home."

Amos watched Hill's reaction, which was to let out a raucous laugh. He was a tall man and his hearty laugh was infectious. Cora was just the opposite in appearance. She sat on the sofa knitting. She was a small woman, which seemed to magnify

Hill's lengthy frame.

Hill shared with Amos how they moved from Alabama to Brooklyn for reasons much like his own. He and Cora had two grown children, Claude and Babe. Claude married his sweetheart Edith Johnson in 1921. Hill also had other children from a previous marriage.

"Well, Rev, we sho' nuf would like to get out the city, though it's a heap better than way we come from," Hill laughed. "But I ain't got the money to buy land right now," he said shaking his head. Amos noticed that Cora smiled and kept knitting.

"Well, I'm sho' you got 'bout much as we had when we come here," Amos said, thinking about how the Lord had blessed him with a new job as a watchman for Duryea Motor Company of Somerville. He now planned to save enough money to buy a few trucks and go into business on his own. "Ya'll welcome to stay at our place 'til you can save enough to buy a piece a property out there," he offered. "I wouldn't charge you no rent. Just help out with the farming and save up some money."

Amos saw Cora put her knitting down. "Tell Frances I'll bring some potato salad on Sunday," she said. She glanced at Hill. Amos was encouraged when they both laughed.

Andrew Murdock, Sr. and Shorty Haynes came north for the promise of steady work on the extensive railroad lines being laid. Amos became fast friends with the young men in his travels into Somerville. Andrew later rented a room in Amos' home.

Frances was shucking corn in the garden one Saturday afternoon when she heard Andrew speaking to a group of young girls. They were walking from General's house towards her home.

"Hey, pretty girls," she heard Andrew speak, "especially you in the middle."

Frances stretched her neck to see who he was talking about. Amanda was in the center. "You sure look nice," he continued.

Well, Frances thought as she looked at Mandi, Loudia, and Babe, *they all pretty.* But she couldn't deny that Mandi was beautiful. She observed her tall, slender niece, and it was easy to see how any man might be taken with her. She was breathtaking. Her skin was the color of honey, and her hair so black that blue highlights appeared to dance around it. She wore her shoulder-length hair piled high in a bun. Wisps of hair fell out of the roll to her long striking neckline.

Hmm, Frances thought, *wonder how General and Vi gonna like this?* As she looked at Mandi's face, she could tell she was smitten with Andrew. *It's a good thing he a nice man,* she thought, *that's why Amos let him rent a room,* she thought. She saw Shorty pull up and get out of his car.

"Hello, ladies," he said with an easy laugh. "Papa Strong messin' with ya'll? He may be strong but he just a big teddy bear deep down."

The girls made their way onto Frances' yard and Mandi asked, "What kind of name is that, Papa Strong?"

"Aw, Murdock got that name down south from the young kids. He so strong he could pull trees up from the ground with his bare hands. I saw him do it many a day."

"I thought I left that name down south along with some other stuff best to be forgotten," Andrew laughed.

"Papa Strong, huh? I kind a like that name," Mandi laughed.

Lord, would you listen to her? Frances thought. She put down the bucket of corn and came to the edge of the garden within sight.

"Oh. Hi, Aunt Frances. We didn't see you back there," Mandi said.

"Lou, Babe, ya'll take this corn to the house for me."

"Yes, ma'am." They picked up the bucket of corn and headed for the house.

As soon as Babe and Lou were out of earshot Frances whispered to Mandi. "He a nice man, but who knows if he settled."

Andrew got in the car with Shorty. "See ya'll later," he called from the window.

Mandi looked dreamy-eyed, but quickly straightened her face as she looked at her Aunt. "Aunt Frances," Mandi said softly, "please don't say anything to Mama and Daddy."

Her words touched Frances. She remembered how she felt when she fell head over heels in love with Amos. "No, I won't say nothing' chil'. I won't have to," she laughed, "'cause you know Vi can read ya thoughts. Lord knows she can."

"Amos, let's get word down to Reverend Bryant in Tye, Tye, Georgia, and have him come up for a spell. I miss ol' Bryant. Don't you? I bet he would love it here in New Jersey," General said.

"I was thinkin' 'bout Reverend Bryant and his family the other day," Amos laughed. "He sho' could make a good livin' up here 'cause he can make anything grow. Erious might think he done died and went to heaven with all this land for crops."

"It sho' would be lots of children out here then. Him and Annis got 'bout nine head a children, I believe," General said.

"Yeah, nine or ten, but we can always make room. Don't care how many it is. The more the merrier. The Lord will always make a way."

General felt the familiar rush of energy that always overtook him when he was about to start building. This time he was getting ready to build another home on his land for his children. He looked thoughtfully at Amos. "Bro', did you ever think we'd be livin' up here and doin' all that we done so far?" General asked. The two sat in the kitchen talking and laughing about their blessings from God. Before Amos could answer, he continued, "I been buildin' houses non-stop since I got here. I remember I was goin' back and forth about buyin' the land, but Vi said, 'You been building houses since I knew you. It's high time you built one for me and these kids.'"

"She sho' was right too," Amos chuckled.

General felt at peace as he talked to his brother. "Hill and Cora sho' done settled in cross the street," he said.

"Yeah, well, they 'bout happy as they can be," Amos agreed. "Everybody just chipped in with all the supplies to build they house. I don't think they had to spend no money at all on materials. Hill was laughin' and goin' on all while that house was being built."

"Yeah. Cora started movin' stuff from your house to the new house way before it was even finished," General laughed, "if it wasn't no more than carryin' pots and pans to the new place. And they son, Claude, well he just a natural born-carpenter. Don't have to measure nothin'. Just eyeball it and gets it right.

"Well, Amos, I got a mind to ask Robert to try to get that property up the street that's for sale. 'cause you know if Erious come, he'll want his own place quick as he can 'cause of the chil'ren."

"Yeah, you right. I'll have Frances to write a letter to him and see if he want to come alone first. Then if he like it here, he can send for his family."

————

In late 1923, Reverend Erious Bryant, his wife Annis, and their children came to New Jersey to stay, one month after receiving the letter Frances wrote them. They lived with Amos for about six months. Erious used his savings from the south and bought the property up the street on Monmouth Avenue. All the men pitched in to build his family home. They worked on the house late into the night after knocking off from their day jobs. The Bryant home was completed in about two months.

————

Meanwhile, the children from the South were trying to adjust to attending school with white children and being taught by Caucasian teachers. Loudia, especially, found one teacher extremely hard to take. She felt hurt as the teacher smiled warmly at the rosy-cheeked students, but eyed her and the other Negro students with under-eyed suspicion.

"You know the rules, Loudia," Ms. Calcutta spoke sharply that day. "If you are late for school you can't go home for lunch."

She heard the loathing in the teacher's voice as she looked at her. *She is one mean woman,* Loudia thought. *Meaner than some of the white folks in the South. I wasn't really late anyway 'cause she was just taking attendance when I got to class.*

"Ms. Calcutta, I ain't had no breakfast and this the first time I been late this year," Loudia spoke up.

"Well, you should have eaten. You're in the eighth grade, Loudia. What do you think will happen if you're late when you get to the high school? You will get detention, young lady. No, you cannot leave the school for lunch today."

Perhaps it was the rumbling of her stomach from hunger, or the fact that she had been dealing with Ms. Calcutta's less than kind attitude for too long, but suddenly Loudia heard herself rebel. "I'm going home to eat lunch. Like I said, I ain't had no breakfast."

"Don't come back here today if you go home," Ms. Calcutta warned. She walked away.

Loudia saw the look of shock on Johnanna's face, her best friend.

"Lou, Ms. Calcutta won't let you in if you leave. You better stay here before you get in trouble."

"Ump, that lady telling me the wrong thing 'cause I'm going home and I'm coming back to school," she vowed. "Tell Nora and the others that I went on to the house 'cause they'll be wondering why I didn't wait for 'em." She could tell by Johnanna's face that she thought she was making a huge mistake.

"Okay, I'll tell them," Johnanna said reluctantly. "But you better hurry up back here, girl, before she figures out you're gone."

Loudia devoured some of her mother's homemade buttermilk biscuits with jelly as soon as she made it home. She washed them down with milk. *Next year I'll be in high school,* she thought. *No more Ms. Calcutta.*

It began to drizzle as Loudia rushed back to school. She attempted to blend into the line of students entering the building after lunch. Suddenly, she heard Ms. Calcutta's shrill voice single her out.

"Loudia, I told you not to come back here if you left," Ms. Calcutta said, and she shut the door in her face.

Loudia wandered around in front of the schoolyard contemplating if she should go home. *No, I better not do that,* she thought, *I'll get in trouble. Maybe I'll go stand in the toilet until the rain stops.* She held her breath as she stepped into the smelly latrine. Soon the stench was so overbearing she couldn't stay for another minute. *I might as well gone on home,* she convinced herself. She ran to Hobbstown in the pouring rain.

The next morning she was on pins and needles as she hurried to school. She figured Ms. Calcutta reported her and she would have detention. As she entered the school she eyed Johnanna waiting for her outside Ms. Calcutta's classroom. Johnanna grabbed her arm and whispered, "Girl, Ms. Calcutta sent me looking for you yesterday because some officials came to the school to visit. She didn't want them to see you standing outside in the rain. Lou, you should have seen her face. She turned white as a sheet when they came to the class. I checked all around for you, but you were gone."

Loudia felt the pleasure of laughter begin at the pit of her belly. By the time it worked its way to her mouth she held her stomach to control an outburst. As Johnanna looked at her with a question, Loudia realized she did not understand why she was so amused. "Girl, I was in the toilet, but I couldn't stay in there. I went on home after a while. But it serves her right for being so nasty."

"So that's where you were when I came looking for you?"

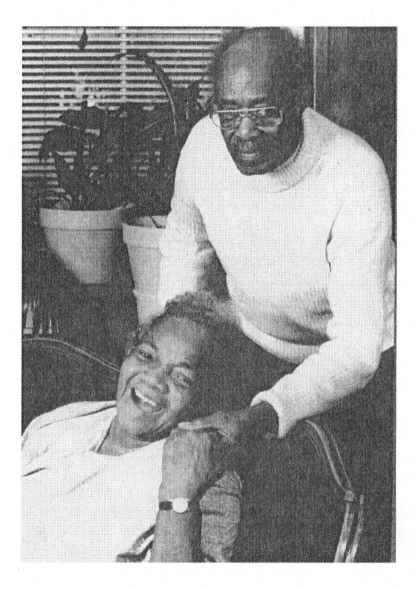

Loudia & John Proctor, Sr.

Johnanna looked incredulous. "I never thought to look there. Ooh, I wouldn't go in that toilet unless I absolutely had to. Well, I bet she won't do that anymore. Lou, I swear, her hands were shaking like a leaf," Johnanna giggled.

As they entered the class Loudia felt Ms. Calcutta's eyes on her.

"Good morning, girls," she said.

Loudia detected a different tone to Ms. Calcutta's voice. She sounded almost kind. She smothered the urge to laugh, and attempted to keep a straight face as she looked at the teacher. "Good morning, Ms. Calcutta."

By 1928, Hobbstown had grown by leaps and bounds as some of the young adults intermarried and formed blood connections within the town. Frances Hobbs completed her child-bearing years with eleven children: Aaron, Amelia, Bertha, Joseph, James, Mary Elizabeth, Frances, Amos, Mattie, Eddie, and Ollie. Reverend Erious and Annis Bryant's surviving children were, Ozelle, Ira, Susan, Sarah Jane, Annis, Theodore Roosevelt (Teddy), Erias (Dobbie), Louis, and Louise.

Claude Miller bought land and built a home on Mercer Street. Mercer was at the southerly end of the town and ran horizontally between Monmouth Avenue and Sussex Avenue. He and Edie settled in with their children. Edie gave birth to twenty-one children. Seventeen survived: William, Evelyn, Ruth, Molly, Paul, James, Esther, Eloise, Anna, Mary, George, Beth, Hannah, Sarah, Naomi, David, and Phillip.

Amanda Hobbs and Andrew Murdock, Sr. were married. They had four children: Mary, Andrew, Jr., Lloyd, and Jean. Joseph Hobbs married Sarah Jane Bryant and two children, Joseph, Jr. and Cornelius, were born from their union. Amelia Hobbs wed Theodore Bryant and their marriage brought four daughters: Juanita (who died as a teenager), Mozelle, Bernice, and Doris. Amelia Bryant died when her girls were young and they were raised by their grandparents, Erious and Annis Bryant. Aaron Hobbs tied the knot with Mamie Miller, daughter of Hill Miller, and they had four children: Lawrence, Aaron, Jr., Cleveland, and Bertha.

———

Howard Holloway skillfully clipped the weeds that grew among the flowers and plants he nursed at the Riley's second home in Florida.

Mrs. Riley spoke to him. "Howard, you know when Mr. Riley and I were up north this last time we noticed that some Negroes from the South are buying property in a little area not far from our home in Somerville. The property is in the Bridgewater area."

Howard ceased cutting and fixed his attention on Mrs. Riley. He thought of how good she and Mr. Riley were to him, his wife Ella, and their daughter Mattie. They gave him a key to their home and stocked it with food for the three months they spent up north each year in their second home. He remembered how he could hardly believe his ears when Mr. Riley handed him the key and Mrs. Riley said, "We want you all to make yourselves comfortable in the house while we're gone. Ella can make sandwiches or whatever you like for lunch while you're working in the yard. All we ask is that you take care of the place and lock up every evening when you leave."

In the six years that he and Ella worked for the Rileys (he kept the grounds and Ella worked in the house as a domestic), he came to the conclusion that they were the best white folk he had ever met. Mr. Riley paid them well and he managed to put away a little something each payday.

Howard stood up as Mrs. Riley continued to talk. He could tell from her lively expression that she was excited, and it was contagious. He eagerly listened.

"You and Ella have been talking about moving north for some time now. I know you would do well up there. There are plenty of jobs available with the railroads being built, and lots of land for gardening. You're both smart people, and I think this would be the perfect opportunity to buy land and build yourselves a home. From what I've heard, a man by the name of Amos Hobbs sometimes rents rooms out of his house to families until they are able to buy."

Howard was touched by her kindness. "I want you to know me and Ella appreciate everything you and Mr. Riley done for us. And, well, if you believe this is a place worth looking at, I'd be a fool not to check into it. Don't rightly yet know how I'll do it, but I got a cousin, John Proctor, and I believe I'll get him to go up north with me, just to look into it."

"That's a grand idea, Howard." He noticed how Mrs. Riley clasped her hands together, a sign that she was deeply pleased. "Yes, I think it's a chance of a lifetime," she continued, "since they said the land is being sold rather cheaply. The people who own it just don't want to be bothered with the upkeep. They can't be asking too much; we actually saw some lots that had large signs saying, 'IOU.' Honestly, nobody deserves it more than you and Ella. And if all goes well we can stay in touch. We'll be right over in the next town for three months out of the year."

"I sure do thank you, Mrs. Riley."

It was 1929. Loudia burst with pride as she watched John Proctor, her husband of a few months, ride through the main street of Somerville in the Memorial Day parade procession. She marveled at how most of Hobbstown, as well as Negro residents of Somerville and the surrounding areas, had turned out for this event. John was now a local celebrity. She smiled and tried to peer over the crowd looking for John's car. Mandi and Nora stood on either side of her.

"John's gone be in the history books," Nora laughed. "Can you imagine, the first Negro to be in a parade in Somerville."

Mandi laughed. "Oh, girl, they won't think it's that

important. Especially since this is just a small town."

"When John first told me his boss asked him to drive one of the cars in the parade I laughed and didn't really pay it no never mind. I just thought he was up to one of his jokes," Loudia said.

"The white folks at the body shop sure must think a lot of John," Mandi commented.

"Oh, yeah, well, you know he's been a mechanic for that body shop for 'bout two years. They let him use the cars. You saw how he sported me around in them sometimes on the weekend," Loudia laughed.

She thought of how she first met John when he came to Hobbstown with Howard and Ella Holloway. Her heart skipped a beat as she remembered how he kind of joked his way into her heart. The Holloways, along with John, were staying in one of the apartments at Uncle Amos' house, and before too long she and John jokingly bantered back and forth.

"You be down here more than you be at your own house," he would say to her.

"And what's it to you," she would shoot back. "This my uncle's house. I can come here whenever I please. And you lucky they let you stay here."

"Aw, girl, don't hand me that," he would laugh. "You know you sweet on me."

She chuckled to herself now, remembering how they had played cat and mouse from the beginning. But soon they were dating. It started when John told her he would help her learn to drive. A warm glow came over her when she remembered how relieved her Uncle Robert was when John began teaching her how to drive.

"Gal, you gone knock down my so-and-so-gate again," Uncle Robert would yell as she came barreling up his driveway determined to learn to drive. And sure enough she would tear it down with the car, time after time. Her uncle would fix the gate each time, seemingly resigned to the fact that she would knock it down again.

"Put ya foot on the break, Doo," (that was the nickname her Uncle Robert gave her as a baby), "BEFORE you get to the gate."

After awhile she noticed he just left the gate down. With that, she felt Uncle Robert was convinced she couldn't learn to drive. As John began to help her with her driving, she saw amusement replace the anxiety that had once besieged her uncle's face when she turned into his driveway. And then one day, to her surprise, she saw that he had put the gate back up. She felt confident then that she would pass the driver's test, and she did.

The roar of the crowd interrupted her thoughts as the motorcade wound down Main Street. "John," she screamed, as she pushed her way to the front through the mass of people. "Hey, John."

He finally spotted her and waved. Her heart melted when she saw the huge smile on his face. As he handled the white 1929 Studebaker convertible with confidence, Loudia thought he had never looked more handsome. Suddenly a thunderous cheer went up from the crowd.

"John Proctor!" they roared. "Hey, John."

Loudia knew this would always be one of the best days of her life.

"Chil' what happened to you?" Vi questioned her daughter as she came in the door with her brother Charlie. Nora's powder blue dress was splattered with mud, and she had her shoes in her hand.

General could see Nora was upset. He jumped to his feet from the sofa where he had been talking with company, Reverend Erious and Annis Bryant. Everyone waited for Nora's response. Of his four children, Nora was the quietest, and General could tell by the way her lips trembled that she was deeply troubled. But time had taught him that with Nora it was better to keep silent and let her tell what had happened at her own pace or else she would clam up. She had been that way all her life.

He remembered how distraught she was in grade school about carrying a bagged lunch to school. She told him that she was embarrassed to eat her biscuits and ham because the white children had deli-cut ham and cheese sandwiches. "Daddy," she said to him shortly after school began that year, "I'm gonna walk home from school for lunch. The white kids make fun of our lunch and stick they tongues out at us."

General thought if it made her feel better then it was alright, as long as she was getting her lesson. And sure enough, unless it was raining, Nora, Loudia, and just about all the kids from Hobbstown walked home for lunch.

He waited anxiously for his youngest child, who was now eighteen, to speak. After a lengthy interval, she did. General could see she fought back tears. He remembered how beautiful Nora looked that morning as she left the house with Charlie. They were headed to a church function and said they would be back in time for a party that night at the dance hall he and Robert built next door to Robert's house. She appeared to have blossomed overnight. There she stood in a powder-blue shirtwaist dress and he wondered where the years had gone. She was a slim fragile child with big beautiful coffee-colored eyes like her mother, and warm brown skin. But above all, he knew that Nora was passionate about the things she believed.

"Charlie was dropping me off at Uncle Amos' house to visit with Mattie for a little bit after we got back. I wanted to show her my dress. So Charlie pulled to the side of the road and I got out of the car. Soon as I got out I stepped into one of those deep ruts on the edge of the street. I fell, and mud splashed all over me. It hit my face and my legs. Just look at my dress. It's ruined. That red mud is hard to get out. The heel broke on my shoe when I fell, and they might as well be thrown away too."

"Lord, look at that dress," Vi said. "Well, it can be washed, baby. It ain't altogether ruined."

General could see Nora was close to tears. She squeezed her eyes shut as if willing the tears not to fall.

"Mother, you know how long it took me to make this dress? I worked on it for weeks. And I saved for these shoes for months. And now everything I'm wearing is destroyed."

"Lord, those was some pretty shoes," Vi said.

Nora held the black velvet t-strap pumps in her hand. General saw everyone look uncomfortably at the hunks of thick mud on the shoes.

"It's a shame," Nora continued. "You have on your Sunday-go-to-meeting clothes and can't even step out of a car out here without getting your belongings destroyed. These roads are terrible. It's bad enough we don't have inside toilets or running water like in the white sections, but why can't they at least fix our roads? Those ruts on the sides of the street have to be at least three feet deep. I'm tired of getting splashed with mud and water. I know I can't be the only one who's sick of it. Can't someone go uptown and complain so they can fix these roads?"

General scratched his head. However, before he could say anything, Reverend Bryant chimed in from his seat on the sofa where he smoked his pipe. "Ya'll know she right," he said. General heard the determination in the Reverend's voice. "I been noticed how they neglect the roads out here."

"Well, they usually come through here and do some repairing every so often," General said, but he knew in his heart it wasn't consistent. He also knew this was the reason the two main roads in the town, Monmouth and Sussex, were in such bad shape. So it didn't surprise him when everyone in the room, especially Nora, met his statement with disagreement.

"Daddy, let me organize a meeting at the house. Just to see if other people out here feel the same way. This way we'll know if the town has the backing of the people before anyone goes to the borough about it."

He looked at Vi for support, but she was silent. She cleared dishes from the table. The truth was, he admitted inwardly, he was tired of the struggle. Although their lives were better now than ever, struggling was all he could remember doing for most of his life. Struggling to help his parents sharecrop, sharecropping for his own family, struggling to make ends meet here in New Jersey, and struggling to ensure they received the bare necessities to keep the town livable. *Lord, I'm tired*, he thought, but he could tell his daughter wasn't. He knew by the intense fire in her eyes that she meant to follow this thing through.

"Gone ahead and have a meeting then," he said. "Might be somethin' good a come out of it."

Nora had just finished wiping the kitchen table when she heard a knock at the door. It was Saturday afternoon and she had been tidying the house all morning to perfection. She took in the spotless front room with a pleased glance and breathed deeply before opening the door.

"Hello, little girl," Annis Bryant greeted Nora. Reverend Bryant was right behind her. A flurry of neighbors came in within the next few minutes: the Millers, Hobbs, Williams, Holloway's, and Reverend Green, who now pastored at Macedonia Baptist Church. Some of the anxiety Nora felt all day began to ease away. She hadn't been confident that sending penny postcards to the families in Hobbstown to discuss the road conditions would bring them out. But now she was elated at the turnout. Her heart raced as she tried to remember what she would say.

"Hello, Ms. Annis and Reverend Bryant. Come on in, everybody. How ya'll doing? Have a seat. Mama and Daddy should be back in a minute. They went over to see Uncle Robert. You know he hadn't been feeling well."

"Well," she heard Uncle Amos clear his throat before speaking. "The town looks good until you sho' nuff look at it hard. Them big beautiful trees give it a nice green look. I believe it was the realtors that planted poplar trees all the way down the main streets back in the early 1920s. But they only last 'bout twenty years since they short-life trees. If you look hard you can see some of 'em look like they withering. We need to start plantin' some long-life trees now so it won't look bare out here in a few years. I just wanted to say that, but I know our purpose tonight is to talk about what can be done 'bout the roads 'cause they in bad shape."

Nora felt her face flush hot because the spotlight was now on her. Her mother's famous words that she had heard since she was a youngster came to mind, *Don't never start nothing you can't finish.* Viola's face now mirrored those words. Nora's heart warmed as her mother smiled at her from the sofa.

"I thank ya'll for coming out today to talk about what we can do about the condition of the roads in Hobbstown. The front and back roads are riddled with those deep ditches and trenches. So many of us have ruined the few nice clothes we have. We shouldn't have to jump over mud and water just to walk the streets when it rains. I think it's disgusting. And even when it's dry, since the streets are dirt, when it's windy and you're walking along dust gets all over your clothes. I believe we need a representative from Hobbstown to go to Borough Hall and tell them what's happening out here. Hobbstown is a part of the township too, and it seems like we're being ignored."

"I'll go." Nora's heart thumped with happiness when Reverend Bryant spoke up. "I'll let them know that people in this community want some action."

As Reverend Bryant communicated his thoughts about the situation, Nora noticed how he placed his ever-present pipe back in his mouth between sentences. "We have a church in the community and a big playground in the park for the children. We need good roads to get around on. I know some of the politicians up at the borough. I'll talk to 'em, whether it works or not."

When others in the room responded in agreement, Nora's

spirits soared. She felt she had accomplished what she set out to do.

Early the next week the Department of Transportation (DOT) came to Hobbstown and Nora then knew the meeting was a real success. The DOT laid red brick sand on Monmouth Avenue and Sussex Street. They also covered the four smaller arteries in the town, Adamsville Road, Hudson Street, Mercer Street, and Henry Street. She watched from a window in her house as they pressed the new sand into the near-bottomless potholes of Henry Street. When they were finished the lane was smooth and hard like cement. The deep holes were gone. Nora was proud of how she rallied the town into taking a stand.

After that incident, the township refurbished the roads every few years. And they later covered the roads with tar for the first time. Nora thought it gave Hobbstown a neat, clean look, more like that of the surrounding communities. By the time they laid the first tar she had eloped and married her sweetheart, Clinton Williams. They moved to Manville.

Amos heard the Beekman Brothers playing their guitars in the dance hall from where he and his brother Moses sat resting in his front yard. It was Friday evening and he was glad to see the sun go down. It had taken all day for them to plow the open field across Henry Street with the help of his horse, Duke. Now it was ready for crop planting. The sorghum cane had come up so nice in New Jersey, but it wasn't like the sugar cane they grew in the South. Still, it served its purpose for sweetening anything. In addition, he grew an abundance of tomatoes, cucumbers, corn, and vegetables, and shared what he could with neighbors and friends.

"Lord knows I'm glad you here, Moses," Amos said to his brother. "Not just 'cause you helpin' me out. I miss you. But it's hard travelin' on all of us, 'specially since things gettin' so expensive. Cost a right smart of money now travelin' by train."

"Yeah," Moses responded, "that's reason I was so glad when John Proctor offered to come get us and drive us back. It saved me plenty money. I can't get him to take a dime except for gas money. Here lately something just kept gnawin' at me. I had to come see 'bout Rilla and Lightnin' and my grandbaby, Ada. But they seem like they all doin' just fine up here. Still, you always gone miss 'em when they way from home, 'specially when they so far away. But I know ya'll gone look after 'em and I can go back south at peace."

"Aw, well we gone look after any of 'em that come up to these parts. Even when they think they on they own we still be watchin' out for 'em and liftin' 'em up in prayer. And you know ya daughter Rilla came up here and seem like she been here all the time. Lord, she keep they place General built on Henry Street spotless. You can 'bout eat off the floor it's so clean. During the week they mostly do day's work for some of the white women up there in the Bridgewater Mountains. Then, come Sunday we all go to church."

"And the church down there wasn't built up like that last time I was here. It looks good."

"Yeah. Macedonia Baptist Church come a long way. We built it after we tore the barn down here next to the house where we used to hold church. The dance hall is still here, though. Here come some of the young people now. Seem like they can hear that music before they start playin' good."

Amos followed Moses' gaze toward the front door of his home as it opened. Mattie came out. She was dressed in a matching skirt and sweater. She walked over to them where they sat relaxing under the big tree in the front yard.

"Look at my baby niece," Moses said. "Just as pretty as a picture."

Mattie bent down and gave him a peck on the cheek.

"Last time I saw you, ya hair was in pigtails and you had on corduroy pants. Now look at you. Got ya hair combed out long and got on a fancy outfit. Must got a boyfriend," he laughed.

Yeah, I reckon so, Amos said to himself as he looked misty-eyed at his daughter. He silently echoed his brother's opinion that she was certainly a pretty girl. She was dating James Mahaffey, or "Dink," as he was familiarly called. He was fond of Dink, and pondered in his heart if perhaps one day the two might be joined at the altar.

"You going next door, baby?" Amos asked Mattie.

"Yes, Daddy. Just for a little while. I won't be late," she said. She put her arms around his neck, kissed him on the cheek, and she was gone.

Amos could hear the familiar sound of big band music as it floated out of the dance hall. It drew patrons like a magnet. And he knew that soon buses from New York would pull up, full of young people eager to get into the dance hall. He drank deeply from the cold lemonade Frances brought them and tried to cool down in the still hot, dusk-dark evening. After setting the glass down by the tree, he looked up to see Lula Bell, a local singer. She was a big woman.

"Hey, Reverend Hobbs, how ya'll doing? We gone shake 'em up in here tonight," she laughed.

"How do?" Amos said. "Ya'll have a good time now."

"Well it can't be nothing but a good time when I sing. That's why folks come from all over," she laughed confidently.

"This my brother Moses, visitin' from south," Amos said.

"Well, hello, Mr. Moses," Lula Bell said, "come on over next door and hear me sing. I promise you'll enjoy yourself."

"Oh, no, ma'am. I'm just gone enjoy myself right out here. Thank you anyhow."

Amos couldn't resist. "Why don't you come to church on Sunday and sing for the Lord," he said. Suddenly, the sassy demeanor left the girl's face. It was replaced by a moment of recognizable melancholy. She then turned and walked away, but glanced back at them as she entered the dance hall.

"Sho' is a lot of cars out here now," Moses said. He sat back down. "The band sound mighty nice."

"Oh yeah, cars a be lined up on every street out here after while; and cars a fill up the park. It's mostly like this every Friday and Saturday night. People come from everywhere to hear the Beekman boys from Somerville play, as far away as New York. Well, it might be one day they'll be coming out here to the church like this. But ain't no harm in 'em having a little fun; that's reason we built the dance hall. I like to see everybody happy and enjoying themselves. Though sometime seem like they don't know when to go home. Amos chuckled inwardly at how the town had grown since his family moved there in 1921.

"Yeah, the town is built up a lot since I been here," Moses said. "Make a person feel right at home."

It was wintertime in the early 1930s. Anna Miller and some of her siblings set out for the mile long walk to school that morning. They took the shortcut behind Macedonia church and crossed over Woodlawn Avenue and met up with some of the other students walking from another direction to the school. It was frigid out and, as they approached the big white colonial school house that was the elementary school, they rushed to the classroom, anxious to warm up. The principal usually came in early and placed coals in the furnace in the basement each day during winter to heat the school. As Anna prepared to remove her coat, she felt the room begin to warm. The teacher helped each child remove coats and ankle-length scarves that were wrapped snugly around their necks, mouths, noses, and heads. Since there were at least 35 kids in the classroom it would take a minimum of half an hour for class to begin. The large room was divided into two classes, kindergarten through fifth on one side, and sixth through eighth on the other.

As Anna took her seat, she saw that the sliding doors, which contained the blackboards and the shades for mathematics was already pulled down. She took out her math homework and studied the shades. There was one shade for each; addition, subtraction, multiplication, and division. If there was one thing she knew, it was that the teachers expected the students to put forth their best effort. They had to work for their grades because one could not move to the next level if they did not earn the grade.

She had grown accustomed to the predominantly white school environment because it was all she had ever known. For the most part, the Hobbstown students got along with the white children, but there were name-calling days. However, the teacher quickly dispelled the taunting by sending the name caller to the principal's office. But Anna realized early on that when the principal heaved coals into the pot-bellied furnace on cold wintry mornings, they received the same warmth as their white peers. And as the teachers taught class, they gleaned the same benefit of exemplary education.

In the 1940s Marian Proctor was in grade school. She hated the frigid winter days of walking to school. As she and her cousins, Doris and Mozelle Bryant, hurried towards Mercer Street, they met Esther and Molly Miller. Molly always sang gospel at the top of her lungs all the way to school. No matter what, when they hit Mercer and Marian heard Molly singing, some kind of peace came over her. To that end, she had learned to pay no heed to some of the bias incidents that befell her at school. However, one happened at the culmination of 8th grade that could not be ignored.

It was 1947. Marian was so excited she could hardly eat the night before her 8th grade class trip to Washington, D.C. She couldn't remember doing anything so thrilling in all of her life. In addition, her cousin, Doris, and Billy Miller, who was also a classmate, would also attend the all-day outing. They were to get up early in the morning to meet the bus, which would leave the school at 6:00 a.m., and would return home that same night.

——

The day had been exhilarating, and jammed pack with things to see. The class took buses to the various memorial sites, the U. S. Mint, and the Arlington Cemetery. Marian, Doris, and Billy made their way to the main dining hall, which had been elegantly prepared for the students. This was to be the highlight of the day.

"You kids come with me," the teacher motioned to them just before the three students entered the dining hall. "You'll have your dinner in another area." She sounded matter-of-fact.

Marian looked around the tiny room to which the teacher brought them and saw there was no one there except the three of them. She couldn't believe it, and as she looked at Doris and Billy she knew they were having a hard time swallowing this blatant slap in the face. *We saved practically all year for this trip and now we can't eat with the white kids. Why not?* she wondered. Her eyes welled with tears.

——

They returned home that Friday night. Marian cried the entire weekend, as she reiterated the story to her family. Loudia was in the principal's office before the first bell rang that Monday morning.

"My daughter Marian, Doris, and Billy Miller paid they money just like the white kids to go to Washington. They made they grade, and they deserved to be treated just the same as the other children. Why wasn't they allowed to sit in the main dining area to eat their dinner like the white kids? They was placed in a separate room to eat by themselves. Marian said they didn't even have the same food as the other kids; that was wrong. Those kids was very hurt by what happened on that trip. That should never happen again."

———

The next year, Marian's younger sister, Sally, was on her way to D.C. for her 8th grade class trip. However, this year the children would be staying overnight. Sally was beside herself with anticipation. She couldn't wait to see what it felt like to be that far away from Hobbstown. It almost felt like she was going to another world. Her cousin Bernice Bryant, who was in high school, would accompany her on the tour. They were both extremely excited since Bernice had not been to Washington either.

Sally was the only Negro in her class. However, she adjusted well to the school environment, mainly because Ms. Havland, her teacher, had sheltered her throughout grammar school.

"Sally, I need to speak to you after class," she said not too long after kindergarten class began that year. She went up to Ms. Havland after class, just a little hesitant.

"Dear, this bag of clothing is for you. Please tell your parents that I gave them to you, okay?"

Sally was happy. She loved clothes, and had already begun learning to sew. "Thank you, Ms. Havland. I'll let my mother and father know. Can I give some to my sisters if they don't fit me?"

Ms. Havland smiled warmly at Sally. "Yes, dear, by all means. There are also some trousers in there that might fit one of your brothers."

So this became the norm between teacher and student during grammar school. Ms. Havland was always giving her something and making her feel special.

Sally was a quick learner academically, and sewing was her passion. By the time she was ready to graduate from 8th grade, she was making most of her clothing for herself and her sisters. Her younger sister Gerri showed the same talent for needlework, and Sally helped her perfect it.

But now she was getting ready to embark on the same trip her sister Marian had taken last year to D.C., which, in the end, had been a disaster.

"You and Bernice make sure to do everything the white students do," her mother advised, "especially eating in the big dining room. The principal assured me last year that what happened to Marian and them will not happen again."

————

Sally was elated on the way back home from the trip that Saturday afternoon. She, Bernice, and some of Sally's white friends talked and laughed the whole time. It had been a wonderful time. And just like her mother said, they were treated just like the white children. She couldn't wait to get home to tell *Muma* and the rest of the family.

Chapter 3

Awakenings

Although Hobbstown was located in Bridgewater, it functioned by and large to itself and seemed the "white elephant" of the township. Nevertheless, the elderly men and women were wise and upstanding, some of the best to ever break bread. They loved their children into loving their brown skin, which helped them deal with adversity at predominantly white Bridgewater Township public schools. And, the social atmosphere of the town kept the younger generation content within the community.

"Cindy, get back from the stove," Nearo scolded his youngest daughter. He scooped her up in his arms. "Daddy's little girl," he cooed in her ear. "You got to stay 'way from there before you get burnt."

Nearo was frustrated that each day seemed to be this child's challenge to get close to the red-hot burning coals in the pot-bellied stove. He knew she was mesmerized by its warmth, but was too young to know how dangerous it could be. He thanked God that somehow one of her older brothers or sisters would catch her in the nick of time. Nearo picked her up now and threw her in the air. She giggled as she tumbled back down to his waiting arms, and he laughed along with her.

As usual when he came home from work, Mary, his wife, and

the older girls were preparing supper. He observed Mary as she dished up food from pots on the stove and he relished the rhythm of this daily routine. It was good to come home to family after a hard day's work at the Singer Construction plant.

Without taking her eyes off the stove, Mary greeted him. "Hey, Nell. The food will be ready in a few minutes."

It struck him that her pregnancy showed. "How you feeling, Mary?" he asked with concern, as she placed a heaping bowl of rice on the table.

He saw that her face was a little drawn as she looked up at him. "Aw, I'm feeling fine, just a little backache, but I'm alright."

"Hi, Daddy," his daughters spoke to him as they set the dinner table. The boys jumped up to greet him and then went back to a game of marbles in the living space of the home.

"Hey, kids, how ya'll doing?" Nearo washed his hands and sat down at the kitchen table to read the newspaper until the food was ready to be served. He savored these quiet moments, especially since he wanted to advance his seventh-grade education by reading the daily paper.

"Boys, wash ya hands and come on to the table," Mary said to George, Nearo, Jr. (Bubba), Litdell (Lit), and Frank (Perk). "Daddy's getting' ready to say grace so we can eat."

Nearo laid the paper on the floor next to his chair, clasped his hands together, and said words of prayer.

"I can't believe we'll be movin' out in a few months," Mary said, as she took in the one big room.

"Yep, and in the new house we'll have inside utilities, a brand new washroom. God has been good, but then he was good when he gave us this place to stay."

It was 1951 and Nearo Williams was about to move his family into a new home at 5 Monmouth Avenue. The place they lived in now had served many families in Hobbstown as home during the interim of building a new dwelling. And their newly built home was located not more than a few stone throws up the street.

However, he could not help but think of what life might have

Nearo Williams, Sr.

been had his first wife, Adele Grace Williams, lived. The couple met and married in Panama City, Florida. They wanted lots of children. He remembered how they prayed that God would bless them with a "quiver full." However, it took eleven years before their first child, Mary Nell, was born. They were ecstatic. The other three children followed in rapid succession; Nearo, Litdell, and Lucinda (Cindy), respectively.

Adele took ill out of the blue with headaches and stomach ailments a few months after she gave birth to their last child. Nearo took her to doctor after doctor. They prescribed medicine, but nothing helped for very long. Within a few months she was nearly bedridden. As he watched her failing health he felt helpless that he could do nothing to ease her suffering. He prayed over her night and day. One evening he came in from his job at the local steel mill to a strangely silent home.

Where are the children? he wondered. They always ran to him when he came home from work. He tiptoed into the bedroom to check on Adele since he knew she was likely resting or asleep. All four children lay sleeping at her head and feet. "Adele," he whispered in her ear. She did not respond. He touched her face and was alarmed at the icy feel to her skin. He picked her up out of the bed and tried to get her to stand up. His thoughts reeled as he wondered what to do. "Adele, wake up, darlin'. Come on now, open your eyes." But there was no breath left in her frail beautiful body.

On that day in 1949 he lost his love, Adele. It shook him to the core with grief even more so because she was just thirty-two years old. He felt the bottom had fallen out of his world, and he was filled with enormous sorrow. *How can I raise my children without a mother?* he asked the Lord. *Lord, shall I go up north with my sisters and brother?* He pondered on reasons to remain in the panhandle, but the reality that he needed family weighed heavy on his mind. Adele didn't have many remaining living relatives. Her mother and father had also gone the way of the earth.

Lemon, her brother and only sibling, died a few years earlier. Nearo thought of his mother, Lucinda. *If she was still living she would help me with the children. But what in the world will Papa Frank do if I leave here?* The South was all his father knew and he realized Papa would not leave Panama City.

Nearo's sisters, Nina, Nolia, and Annie Kaye, had moved north in the mid-1940s. His younger brother, Chester, completed a stint in World War II with the Armed Services. After leaving the military, Chester and his wife, Helen, had joined the sisters in New Jersey.

"I'm sure gone miss ya'll," Papa Frank said. A weight had lifted off Nearo's shoulders when Papa Frank gave him his blessings to leave Florida. "But I believe it's best for the kids. Ya sisters can help you tend to the chil'ren once you get a job up there. Ya'll gone be alright son. And I can visit every so often."

So with a heavy heart and four children stair-stepping at his knees, Nearo left the south and settled in the North in 1949. He later married his second wife, Mary Elizabeth Simpson Wright. She hailed from Sneads, Florida, and had come north eager for a better life, too. Mary was divorced with four children: George, Mearce Dee (Dee), Lena, and Frank, respectively. And so they became one family.

It was 1955 and Mary heard a knock on the front door of their home. When she opened the door the familiar frame of her brother-in-law, Johnny Butler, filled the doorway.

"How ya'll doing this morning, Mary? The milkman just left," he said. Johnny handed her four jugs of milk. "Hey, yella gal," he laughed as he picked Diane up and swung her in the air. Johnny was tall, light-skinned, and round while his wife, Nolia, was dark, short, and petite.

"She's getting just as big, about to catch up with Cindy," he said. Mary smiled as he pulled Cindy's pigtails affectionately. "How old is Diane now?" he asked.

Mary laughed and smoothed the bedspread on the sofa one last time before she looked up at Johnny and spoke. "Oh, she's three now. Yeah, she growing like a weed. Trying her best to keep up with Cindy. Them other girls went down to the park. They got softball practice this morning. Way Nolie? At the house?"

"She went to the grocery store right quick. Nearo ain't here? I told him last night I was coming over to help him fix that leak in the bathroom." He sat down on the couch. Mary tried not to look anxious as the sofa sagged in the middle.

"The house sure look nice. It's so neat you can eat off the floor. How you do it with nine kids? Shoot, it's just Nolie and me and darned if ya'll place don't look better than ours."

"Well, the children help out a lot," Mary laughed. "They all got chores to do 'cause we have to have a clean house, especially since we built this house from the ground. All that hard work we did to get in here, too. Remember how we worked on it sometime late into the night? You and Nell would rig up them lights so we could see." Mary smiled now as she thought of how she helped sheetrock the house although she was pregnant at the time.

"Yeah, well we wanted to hurry up and get finish before you had the baby. And it wasn't long after ya'll moved in that you had Diane," Johnny grinned. "You know the ranch we live in now is the third house I built out here, not counting laying the foundation for this house."

Mary could tell Johnny was getting excited as he did whenever the conversation turned to building. She had marveled at how he and Nell read a blueprint without any training, and Johnny laid bricks better than anyone she had ever seen. He was quick and efficient and had put down the foundation to their home in just a few days.

"You want some coffee, Johnny? I got a fresh pot on the stove.

Nell and the boys should be back here soon. They went to the store. I thought they'd be back by now."

"No thanks. I had some before I left the house."

It crossed Mary's mind that Johnny was a good brother-in-law. *Lord knows,* she thought, *he couldn't have worked harder on this house than if he was building it for himself.*

She got the broom from the kitchen and swept the living room floor while Johnny talked. "Don't seem too long ago that Nolie and me lived in the two-family I built across the street from our ranch house. Remember when Chester and Helen moved out here from Manville? We put that house up at 14 Monmouth pretty quick for them, too."

"That's right. Helen was pregnant with Chester, Jr. Oh, that sound like Nell 'n' them out there now," Mary said, as the familiar sound of Nearo's red pickup truck pulled into the driveway. She opened the door and stood to the side as her four boys rough and tumbled their way into the house. Nearo was right behind them.

"Hey, Johnny," Nearo said. Mary could hear the fondness in his voice. "Sorry I ran late. Me and the boys went to the hardware store to pick up some plumbing supplies. So happen we ran into Reverend Hobbs at the store and we got to talkin'."

"Oh, yeah? I talked with him and General down at Duke's Pasture a few days ago," Johnny said. "I was telling them how it seemed like fate when Nolie and me met Clinton and Nora Williams while we was working at the supply center in Raritan during the war. They both worked there, too. So happen we all was living in Manville then. But almost every day at the packing plant Clinton talked about this place called Hobbstown. He's the one that brought me out here to look at some property after I told him I was a mason and was looking for land to build a house."

Mary listened to their chatter while a thousand chores that needed to be done ran through her mind. She breathed a sigh of relief that it was Saturday and a light dinner was the norm. The more she thought of all that needed to be done the more anxious she became for the time when the older girls would come through the door to help with what appeared to be never-ending household tasks. The men's voices seemed to rise and fall with the rhythm of her thoughts. She pulled out the canning supplies in the kitchen.

"Hobbs was telling me they had another brother, Robert, that lived here too, and died in 1942," Nearo spoke. "Some kind of stomach ailment got to him. Then he said his wife Frances died in 1945. Did you know Booker T. and Leona Tukes is related to Hobbs? Well, they call her Nonie. He told me Nonie's mother is his niece; said her name is Lizzie."

"Yeah, well it seem like just about everybody out here is related in some way. Booker T. and Nonie got lots of children too. I believe it's nine of 'em. Nice kids. Since they been living in the two-family I know all they names: Lizzie, Helen, Gladys, Priscilla, Rosie, Betty, Henry, Tom, and Booker, Jr. Seem like I can remember the names of these children out here so well."

"Doggone it!" Nearo yelled. Mary stopped what she was doing and went to the living room door.

"Nell, what's wrong?"

"It's alright, Mary," he said. "I just remembered I left my good wrench at Reverend Bryant's house the other day when I was doing some plumbing on his sink. Come on with me, Johnny, cross the street. Then we can come back here and get started."

"Alright, but let's hurry and come on back. I told Nolie I'd be back to the house in time for lunch."

———

"Mary, you 'bout ready?" Daddy asked Mama. He walked down the hallway of their home. Cindy could tell he was excited because he kept mentioning how Uncle Chet was looking for them to come to Three Towers that Friday night. This was some kind of fancy new supper club where Uncle Chet brought in singing acts. Daddy said Uncle Chet was "gettin' to be well-known as a talent scout."

"Chester said he'll save us some good seats," Daddy's voice carried to the bedroom, as Mama entered it after leaving the bathroom. All the girls were helping Mama prepare for the big evening. Mama was beautiful, but tonight Cindy thought she looked like a radiant near-white doll. Her smooth skin was the color of cream and her long midnight curls hung to her shoulders in perfection. She thought of how Mama wet her hair with a comb and eventually emerged with a head of beautiful dangling curls. She had gotten used to hearing black folks refer to Mama's hair as "good hair," and came to understand this meant it didn't frizz when it got wet. To the contrary, Mama combed her locks with water and carefully parted it into small strands. She then oiled each strand with Royal Crown hair pomade and rolled each piece upward with her two index fingers pressed together. When she was finished the hair framed her pretty face like a halo.

As her older sisters fluttered around Mama helping her dress, Cindy and Diane sat on the bed and watched every move. Mama smoothed Evening in Paris face powder on with a small sponge as she peered at her image in the dresser drawer mirror. Dee laid Mama's sky-blue silk dress on the bed. Lena held the matching long-sleeved, bead embroidered jacket to her chest as if she were wearing it.

"Oh, this is so pretty," Lena said. She spun around with the jacket.

Mama slipped into the beautiful dress. On her slim frame the hem hit her leg at the calf. "Chil', hand me the jacket. Daddy's waiting on me."

Lena handed Mama the jacket, and she quickly put it on. Mary Nell pulled Mama's new high heels from the closet and handed them to her. They were shiny black patent leather, with an opening in the front that displayed the tip of the big toe. The shoe was completed with a thin strap that wrapped around the

Mary Williams

ankle. Mama slipped into the pumps and picked up her bottle of Evening in Paris perfume. When she sprayed both sides of her neck the room lit up with the familiar pleasant fragrance.

"Now, I want ya'll to stay to this house and no company," Mama said. "I mean nobody leave from here. Alright, I'm ready," she said. She smoothed her dress and glanced in the mirror one last time before leaving the room.

In the bright light of the living room Mama's hair danced to its own song. As she stood next to Daddy, Cindy thought they must be the most beautiful couple in the world. Daddy was tall, dark, and slim, but with her high heels on Mama could look him in the eye.

"Mary, how this suit look?" Daddy asked Mama. "This the one Town Shop dropped off last week, but I ain't had time to try it on until tonight to see 'bout the tailoring. How it fit?"

Cindy watched with interest as Daddy opened the buttons on the double-breasted black suit jacket and pulled it back. She could see the crisp white tailored shirt underneath and the neat-fitting black pants.

Mama laughed and her delicately painted lips parted to reveal even white teeth. "Nell, the suit look fine. They hemmed them just right. We better go. Nolie and Johnny probably there waiting on us. Helen, too."

"Okay, I'm ready," Daddy said. However, Cindy knew that whenever he and Mama were dressed to the nines they wanted their opinion on how they looked. She waited for the words she loved to hear. "How we look, kids?"

"Ya'll look sharp," came the children's collective response.

"Alright, ya'll behave now. George, you in charge," Daddy said.

As soon as the door shut behind their parents, the children went into action. They scurried towards the kitchen to pull out chairs into the living room. Skeeter Boy, a cousin on Mama's side of the family, had come to stay with them for a spell. He was the same age as Lit, eleven, and the two of them together was a barrel of fun. It came to her that they had plenty of folding chairs because they always had big Sunday dinners with loads of relatives. That's when Mama's family from Newark came out to the country and they cooked up a storm: hog maws, chitlins, pig's feet, fried fish and chicken, collard greens, cornbread, and all kinds of cakes and pies.

"Here's the sheet to drape the pulpit," Dee said, and handed it to Bubba.

The boys pulled Daddy's podium from the bedroom to the center of the living room. He was studying to be a minister at St. Paul's Baptist Church in Somerville, and bought the stand along with a tape recorder to practice sermons. Skeeter Boy walked to the makeshift pulpit. The rest of the children took seats in the chairs they had lined up like church pews. Anticipative giggles scattered throughout the room. In one hand Skeeter Boy carried Daddy's bible. He opened the book and placed it in the center of the stand. In the other hand he held one of Daddy's neatly-folded white handkerchiefs. He placed the hankie on one side of the bible.

"Dear Lord, we gathered here today, now, ah, to bless yo' mighty name, now," Skeeter Boy began.

"Yes, Lord," the others shouted, clapping their hands as they had done so many times in real church.

"I said we here to praise yo' almighty name," Skeeter Boy continued. He picked up the hankie and dabbed his forehead like the pastor did on Sunday mornings, then laid it back down.

"Preach, Pastor, preach," resonated throughout the room. They stood and waved their hands to the ceiling.

"That's alright." Cindy blurted out words she didn't understand, but had heard so many times during church service. She threw her hands up toward heaven and mimicked the sisters of the church. As she looked at Skeeter Boy she could tell he was caught up with the lively reception. He walked back and forth in front of the podium and he truly appeared as if he was in the heat of a sermon.

"What you gone do when the well run dry?" he asked loudly, shaking his head from side to side. "You better get to know Him. Ah, I said, you better get to know Him now."

"Yes, suh. Yes, suh," they all chimed in.

The room exploded with laughter as Skeeter Boy went into his full whooping it up mannerisms.

"And a, um, yeah, um. I say, yeah now. He's alright."

A sudden knock on the front door sent the children reeling toward the back rooms. *It's wrong to play church,* Cindy thought, *and now the devil himself is coming to get us.*

"Who is it?" George raised his voice through the closed door. Cindy shivered behind a bedroom door.

Bam, bam, bam. The person knocked harder.

"I said who's there?" George asked again.

"It's Reverend Bryant."

A collective sigh of relief went through the house. George opened the door a crack.

"I just came to check on ya'll. Saw ya Mama and Daddy leave out earlier and told 'em I'd keep an eye out. Everything alright?"

"Oh, yes, sir, Reverend Bryant. We're fine."

"Alright then. Well, good night now."

"Good night, Reverend Bryant."

"Get ya fresh fruit he-ah, fresh vegetables."

Nearo heard Mr. Maja's routine cry that Saturday morning. The soothing sound of his phlegm-filled voice was a regular occurrence on Saturday at sunrise in Hobbstown, and again at midday. Nearo had come to expect it as much as Bob Tail's crow that woke him at daybreak.

Mr. Maja sold vegetables and fruit from his rundown, pea-green bus. However, except for its dilapidation and color, the bus was the spitting image of the yellow school bus that picked up the children at Monmouth Avenue and North Bridge Street.

Maja lived next door to Johnny and Nolia, across the street from Chet and Helen. The peaceful rise and fall of his call for customers was filled with a bottomless rhythm. For a moment Nearo felt he could tap his fingers to it with ease. He heard Mary in the kitchen preparing breakfast.

"Mary, you need anything from Maja?"

"No I don't believe so, not with all the vegetables we picked from the garden. Me and the girls gone do some freezing today."

"Well, I'm gone go out and speak to Maja for a minute."

"Alright, Nell. We'll have breakfast ready in a little bit. Tell Maja hello."

"Okay."

Nearo chuckled as Maja eased his large frame down the steps of the bus. He enjoyed talking to Maja because he was always high-spirited. His infectious laugh drifted through the door with the familiar simplicity that Nearo had come to expect. Maja was a round tall man, coffee-colored, with big sad-sack eyes. When he laughed the deep ridges in his bald head vibrated from front to back, and his body shook like a bowl of chocolate-colored Jello.

"How you doing this mornin', Maja?"

"Mornin', Nearo. Aw, I'm feeling right good this mornin'. Just thanking God to be alive. How ya'll doing? How the family? Hee-haw," deep cough. "Hem."

"Pretty good, Maja. Everybody doing fine, bless God. Mary said to tell you hello. Seem like you earlier than usual this mornin' ain't it?"

"Hee, sho' is. Got to go do some vegetable pickin' this mornin' in Trenton. It's a big farm down there with potatoes and all types a vegetables. Got to...hem," cough, cough, "get it whilst I can."

"That's the truth," Nearo agreed. "Well, I'll take some candy for my chil'ren Maja."

"Sho'. What kind you want?"

"Well, just give me a bunch of penny candy. With a house full

90

of chil'ren you can't give one without giving to the other."

"Well, now that's the truth, Nearo."

The candy was stocked in the front of the bus between a few boxes of produce. Maja went in and came down the steps wiping sweat from his forehead with one hand. In the other he carried a handful of assorted sweets.

"How much I owe you for the candy?"

"That a be twenty-five cents."

"Alright then, Maja. Thank you. Have a nice day now. And take care of that cough."

"Yes, suh, hem," cough, cough, "I will. Now ya'll have a good day too. I'll be back through heh in the evening."

The Hobbstown Park swarmed with activity that Saturday afternoon when Louise Bryant, Cindy Williams, and Helen Tukes arrived. The girls were barely months apart in age. Some of the older Hobbstown girls were in a heated softball game, Naomi Miller, Teresa and Gerri Proctor, Connie Hobbs, Linda Murdock, Lizzie Tukes, Trish Bryant, and Cindy's older sisters. Sometimes they played mothers against daughters or fathers against sons. However, today they were in an aggressive practice game with some of the Somerville girls, who were also on the team. The combined team would play the Carteret girls the following weekend. Mary Nell was at bat.

"Hit that ball, Mary," the crowd shouted.

Pow came the rock-solid sound of ball meeting bat. Mary Nell sailed around the bases with a home run.

Some of the adults were taking the game in lawn side. As she glanced over at the grown-ups, Cindy saw Grandma Fennie, Mama's mother, wearing her familiar straw hat. She rose from her chair when Mary Nell hit the ball.

"Yeah, that's how to do it," Grandma Fennie yelled. "You got to get ugly to play ball," she encouraged the home team. "Ya'll can't play no ball being cute."

All of that practicing had paid off, Cindy thought. Nearo played baseball at school and he and Mary Nell would sometimes practice various throws for hours in the yard. As for herself, she enjoyed watching the game, but wasn't a natural softball player.

The girls' softball manager was Richard Nelson of Somerville. He had an early tie with the men of Hobbstown. As a popular mason he worked with some of them on building jobs in and around the area. Nelson signaled the girls in the outfield to back up. The Somerville girls were up and Rea Vessels was one of the heavy-hitters. Rea swung the bat hard, and the ball vaulted through the air near second base. Linda caught it with ease and hurled the ball to first base where Dee gloved it and touched the base for a quick out.

———

Swoosh. The sound of a basketball dunked in a pick-up game between the neighborhood boys on the blacktop was in full gear.

"Show me what you got," Phil challenged, as he jumped up and slammed the ball into the basket. The others scrambled for a rebound. Lit, Perk, and Nearo were engaged in a do-or-die horseshoe game with some of the Somerville boys. Suddenly, Franks' soda truck rambled down the street on its way to the Holloway home for a delivery.

"Hey, I have a quarter. Wanna go to Ms. Holloway's for soda?" Cindy asked her friends.

Reverend Hobbs sat on his porch as the girls neared his house on their way down the street to Holloway's. "How ya'll?" he asked.

"Hi, Reverend Hobbs."

Whew, Cindy thought, as they went farther down the street. *I smell the pigs.* But sometimes the sweet smell of the cane that Mr. Holloway grew overpowered the odor of the hogs. And when the cane was ripe to the color of banana-yellow, he would sometimes let them pick a few stalks. *Maybe he will let us pick some cane today.*

Adele Williams

Mr. and Mrs. Jenkins sat on their front stoop. "Hey, girls, how ya'll doing today?" Ella Jenkins asked. She fanned herself as she talked.

"Hi, Mr. and Mrs. Jenkins."

"Ya'll come back and get some watermelon," she insisted. "Jenk just bought a bunch of 'em from Maja." Mr. Jenkins twitched his face into a familiar grin.

When they made it to Mercer Street, and the area of the pig troughs, a crowd had gathered. Sure enough, the smell lifted when they came close to the area where the pigs dwelled. But somehow she felt this was not going to be a cane-picking day.

"Gone be a pig shoot," one of the men shouted.

Mr. Holloway ran alongside the pigs with a long-barreled gun by his side. As Cindy watched the pigs run for their lives toward the feeding station, she was both mesmerized and caught off guard. Their shrieks pierced the warm sunny sky, ominously final, pleading for a savior. The animals crashed madly into one another; some fell and were promptly trampled by their peers who writhed in hysteria. She fixed her eyes on Mr. Holloway as he found his target. He lifted the gun and aimed. The shot rang out to objectionable squeals and one pig fell to the ground never to rise again. As the remaining herd of swine snorted and moved in slower fashion the crowd broke up. Although the pigs escaped the fate of landing on the huge barbecue pit at the park that day, the darkness of their destiny loomed in the air like a heavy storm.

The following Tuesday evening, Cindy was in the living room finishing homework when she heard a knock on the front door.

"Come on in," Mama called from the kitchen to the person behind the unlocked door. Daddy had knocked off early from work. He and Mama were in the kitchen. Aunt Helen entered the house, and Cindy could see she looked upset.

"Hi, Aunt Helen."

"Hello, dear," Aunt Helen responded, but quickly went to the kitchen.

"Well, you might as well know now. I went out to Green Knoll School today and gave them a piece of my mind," she said to Mama and Daddy.

"What's wrong, Helen?" Mama asked. "Sit down. Let me pour you a cup of coffee."

"If they think they can treat my son any kind of way they better darn well think again."

"Calm down, Helen," Daddy said, but Cindy could hear the concern in his voice. "Now what happened? Chet was in a hurry when he stopped by here earlier and we never did get the full story. Is Chester, Jr. alright?"

"Yeah, well I guess he's okay now. But when he got off the school bus yesterday he ran all the way home crying. One of the little white girls in his class had a birthday party during school. The girl's mother brought in cake and ice cream for the kids in her class, but the teacher made Chuck leave the room and go to another class. You know he's the only black student in his class. He's just a little third grader for goodness sake, and of course he didn't understand why they made him leave the room."

"Yes, well all of 'em just about the only black in they class," Mama said. "It's just a few of 'em in the whole school."

"Chuck said they took him to another class until the party was over. When they brought him back to his regular class he asked the girl why he couldn't stay for the party, and she said, 'Because you're from Hobbstown and you're colored.'

"But what hurt me so bad was he asked me why white people don't like him because he's colored. That thing really got to me. All I could do was sit down in a chair and cry. Then I got mad. So I went over there today and told that principal how bad they hurt my son. He had the nerve to say he didn't know anything about it. Talking about he was sorry and would speak to the teacher to make sure it never happened again. Nearo, I mean I looked him dead in the eye and told him, 'Don't make me come back to this school about these prejudiced behind teachers because I will turn this school out.'"

"Naw, you didn't, Helen?" Daddy questioned. He sounded shocked, but also a little amused. Cindy smiled inwardly because if anyone could set the record straight at school or anywhere else, it was Aunt Helen.

"Oh yes, I did too. And I meant every word."

As she listened to the conversation coming from the kitchen Cindy felt profoundly sad, but at the same time proud of Aunt Helen. However, her words made it clear that the color of their skin was no cause for celebration.

———

By the time she was eleven years old, Cindy understood that her world was totally different from that of her white schoolmates. Although some of the white students were friendly, she found there were others who behaved as if their skin would get dirty if they touched her. There was an unmistakable wall of indifference towards the black students from Hobbstown. While they were educated alongside Bridgewater's wealthy white students, there were also a small number of white students at the school who echoed the same economic status as her family. Those were the students that she felt most comfortable with, although Greta was the exception.

Greta's family was affluent, (she lived in Martinsville) but she and Cindy had been best friends since second grade. Bonnie, and Doreen were her other white friends and they both lived in Bradley Gardens. However, after fifth grade Greta's family moved back to Canada when her father accepted a transfer. The two bawled their eyes out at the end of that school year and vowed to remain best friends and stay in touch. But the many miles between them saw that promise dissipate with all the swiftness of a crumbling sand dune.

After Greta moved away, Bonnie, Cindy, and Doreen were like

the *Three Musketeers* during school hours. They had fun together, but Cindy understood her relationship with them was kin to a nine-to-five job. Outside of school there was little, if any, communication between them. And the less affluent white children more or less received the same treatment from the trendsetters as did the Hobbstown students. They, too, lived on the island of misfits since they lacked the prerequisite of gorgeous clothes and ready cash for any adolescent financial whim.

"Hi, Ms. Mott. Here's the cup of sugar Mama said to bring you."

"Okay. Thanks, Cindy. You want a slice of apple pie? Sit down." Ms. Modestine said.

She sat at the Bryant's kitchen table on Hudson Street, located behind Reverend and Annis Bryant's home, waiting for Louise and her older sister, Latricia (Trish), to finish dressing. The sisters had three brothers, Robert, Wade and Charles, respectively. Their father was Louis Bryant, one of Reverend Erious and Annis Bryant's sons, who married Modestine Dunlap. It was a warm Saturday afternoon and the girls were going to the Hobbstown park for a scavenger hunt. There would also be a pig roast.

"Yes, thank you," Cindy responded, as Ms. Mott placed a piece of pie in front of her at the table. As she took the first bite the buttery thick crust melted in her mouth. "Um, this is so good," she said. Ms. Mott made the best apple pie.

"Ya'll girls need to learn how to do more cooking and baking," Ms. Mott laughed.

Trish came into the room with Louise at her heels.

"Hey. Ya'll ready to go?" Cindy asked.

"Yep, we're ready. Helen wants us to stop by and pick her up on the way," Louise said.

"Thanks for the pie, Ms. Mott."

"You're welcome. Trish and Louise, ya'll come on up the street before dark now. You hear me? Cindy, that goes for you too. I know Mary want you back up here before nightfall."

"Yes, Ms. Mott."

"Alright, Momma," Trish said. She sounded eager to go.

"Oh, we need something to put all the stuff in," Louise remembered. She pulled out brown paper bags from behind the refrigerator. They then walked the short distance to the Tukes' property where Helen met them at the door.

"I'm ready," she said.

Her older sister Lizzie stood in the doorway. "I hope one of you wins the contest. Don't spend too much time searching for one thing. Go on to the next item on the list if you can't find something," she said. "I'll be down there later for the cookout."

"Bye."

When they neared the park, they saw Cheryl and Leslie Murdock, Lorraine and Shelby Grey, and Joyce and Ian Gould jumping hopscotch on Monmouth Avenue. The sun-parched road sizzled as misty vapors gave it away, and tiny bubbles of tar burst open in despair. Most of the older teens played *Mother May I* on the blacktop in the park. Lena was *Mother* that day. Across from the park on Sussex Street ropes clicked as Gerri Proctor, Connie Hobbs, Ruby and Betty Stewart, Linda Murdock, and Marie Middleton jumped double-dutch as if for their very survival.

The familiar smell of home-cooked food mixed with mingling happy folk gave Cindy a safe warm feeling. Smoke billowed from the handmade brick pit as some of the men turned the split hog on the grill. They basted it with thick red barbecue sauce. Suddenly there was a loud *clang*, metal hitting metal, the sound of a cowbell. Reverend Hobbs stood on the blacktop beckoning their attention. The park came to a speedy hush.

"How ya'll doing?" he asked. "We'll we gettin' ready to start our annual scavenger hunt put on by Macedonia church. As ya'll know, no one over fifteen can participate. All ya'll young ones need to get the list from the women over there. Now you got a half hour to come back with the things on the list. But you can't go past Adams' Lane to find them and you can't go inside a house. If you do, you disqualified. The one that bring back everything, or most near everything, wins a free ticket to the next Coney Island trip."

Cindy looked at the items on the sheet of paper and was stumped. Some of the stuff could be found along the landscape, like flowers, strawberries, cans, and red dirt; but others, such as soap and hairpins, would likely be in the home. Suddenly a light came on in her head. Her friend Joyce Hobbs lived on Henry Street down from the park with her parents, Charles and Valerie Hobbs, and her 13 siblings. Besides Joyce, she was most familiar with Connie and Ken. She spotted Joyce as she stood reading the list and went over to her.

"Hey, Joyce, let's look on your porch for soap and hairpins. We can probably find that other stuff outside."

Joyce laughed. "Oh, girl, I got hairpins in my head," she said, as she pulled a few out. "Come on. Let's see if we can find some soap in the back. Grandpa General brings home different stuff from the white people in town."

The two searched the area high and low, even combing Joyce's Aunt Loudia's porch and backyard. Their house was a stone's throw away from Joyce's family. Time drew near, but they had no soap, although they had managed to find most of the other items on the list. But a girl from out of town had everything on the list and won the contest. Rumors swirled that she had brought a bag of goodies from home and hid it in the bushes.

It was 1959, summertime, and school was out. Hobbstown's youth had completed a record-breaking track and field day at Calco Park in Bound Brook. This was an annual competition against other surrounding recreational parks. They had captured first place awards in each track and field event under the guidance of James Sermons, the new park director for Hobbstown Park. Some of the sports they competed in were broad-jump, base running, volleyball, relay races, softball, baseball, and archery. They practiced vigorously each summer in anticipation of the high-energy, fun-filled day. The games at Calco included all of the hot dogs, hamburgers, French fries, soda, and ice cream that one could eat for free.

Although Hobbstown had always excelled during the Calco games, they seemed to reach a higher level of athleticism when Mr. Sermons took the reigns. He lived in Somerville and was the brother of Evelyn Field, who resided in Hobbstown on North Bridge Street with her husband and two children. Ms. Field had been one of the first recreational directors at the Hobbstown Park. In addition, her husband, Amos Field, became the Somerville Recreational Department director.

———

Cindy listened with interest that day, along with Hobbstown friends, as Mr. Sermons gave them a pep talk at the park. He was a handsome, brown-complexioned tall man, who seemed to enjoy laughter. However, it was clear that he took his job seriously and expected them to shine.

A large sign had been placed in the park a few months earlier by the Bridgewater Borough, which read Somerville Manor. As she read the name, Cindy wondered if that meant the town was no longer going to be called Hobbstown.

"Boys and girls, Hobbstown is going to Forest Lodge," Mr. Sermons said to the group of youngsters.

Well, I guess we're still Hobbstown, she thought.

"The bus will pick us up at the park next Friday for a field trip to Forest Lodge. Boys and girls, I want you all to be on your best behavior. This is a very important trip for Hobbstown."

The day felt suddenly dreary as Cindy remembered what her sister Mary Nell went through on a class trip to Forest Lodge in eighth grade. Mary Nell came home from the outing with her self-esteem shattered. And then there were all of the other heartbreaking firsts she endured during her years at

Bridgewater High. Somerville High bursts at the seams with students from Somerville as well as Bridgewater. To accommodate the township's rapidly increasing population, in 1958 Bridgewater built its own high school, Bridgewater-Raritan West High School. Mary Nell was the first in the family to attend the school, starting in her sophomore year. Dee and Lena continued at Somerville High since they were closer to completing their senior year.

On the day Mary Nell came home from Forest Lodge, her beautiful face was etched in sorrow.

"What happened?" Cindy asked, as they sat on the edge of their beds later that night.

"I should have known something wasn't right when the teacher told me she would need to find out from the Forest Lodge officials if they would allow me on the premises. But I wanted to go because my white friends talked about how much fun it was to swim in the pools at this beautiful placed called Forest Lodge. So Mama signed the permission slip, and I gave it to the teacher. The next day the teacher told me that, 'Yes, they do allow Negroes inside the resort.' I was so happy I was floating on air."

"They let you in so that means they aren't against us being there, right?" Cindy asked.

"Well, they let me in, but I sure wasn't welcome. Although some of my white friends were with me, there were busloads of kids from other school districts that were not used to being around us. They stared at me like I was from another planet; they whispered and laughed. Eyes followed my every move. I was totally unprepared for the way I was treated. I guess I thought things would be different, better. But instead I stood out like a sore thumb, being the only Negro there. Today was the longest day of my life and the worst. Just because the law said I could go didn't mean they had to accept me. And they didn't."

"Do you all understand?" Mr. Sermons' deep voice penetrated the air like water rushing down nearby Peter's Brook, and Cindy

James Sermons

stopped daydreaming. "I want each of you to bring a signed permission slip from your parents on next Wednesday. The bus will pick us up here at the park at 8:00 a.m. sharp next Friday, so be on time. We'll talk more about the trip next week when you turn in your consent forms. Don't forget. You won't be able to go unless I have a signed permission slip from all parents. Alright kids, I'll see you next week."

"Bye, Mr. Sermons."

"Hey, let's go over to Ms. Georgia Mae's to buy some ice cream," Louise said to Cindy and Helen.

"I didn't bring money with me," Cindy said. The wind had been knocked out of her with this Forest Lodge advent. She didn't want ice cream. "I'll wait here in the park until ya'll come back."

"Okay. We'll be right back," Louise said. She and Helen took off running the twenty-five feet or so to Ms. Georgia Mae's house on Sussex Avenue across from the blacktop.

No one else seems worried about going to Forest Lodge, she thought. She kicked rocks on the side of the street. *I really don't have to go. I could always say I'm sick.* She concentrated on how she might get out of it gracefully. Still, something within her longed to see Forest Lodge. She comforted herself with the fact that this time there would be more than one black person at Forest Lodge.

The bus driver picked them up promptly at the park that Friday morning at 8:00 a.m. He then drove to Bradley Gardens where some of Hobbstown's white schoolmates boarded the bus. Soon they were on their way for the forty-minute ride to Forest Lodge. Although there were about fifteen black children on the bus, Cindy still couldn't shake the jitters. She looked at Mr. Sermons. He didn't appear concerned at all.

"Stay close to one another and to me," he said as they approached the resort. Slowly, but surely, Cindy felt the butterflies abandoning her belly.

"Look at those pools," Shelby exclaimed, as the bus pulled into the Forest Lodge lot. She sat in a seat with her sister, Lorraine. Louise and Cindy were seated right behind them.

Cindy too peered out of the window and saw several oval-shaped, sky-blue pools. "Oh, they're beautiful. Look how blue the water is," she marveled. "Let's get in the biggest one first."

Everyone laughed and piled out of the bus. Mr. Sermons led the way from the bus to the park, and the familiar smell of grilling hotdogs and hamburgers serenaded the air.

"Stay with me," Mr. Sermons directed them. "And we are going to behave like the young boys and girls that your parents raised, right?"

"Yes, sir."

The morning was hot and sticky as they carried their paper bags with a change of shorts and personal items. Mr. Sermons handed a paper to the sour-looking male attendant who took the pass. They walked into the park. Suddenly, the morning chatter of the people in the park came to a grinding halt. Only the sound of the sizzling grills could be heard. Things seemed to shift to slow motion as everyone stared at them.

"Keep moving to the bath house," Mr. Sermons turned and said to them, as if sensing their anxiety. "Good morning," he spoke merrily to a man and woman who stood gawking. As Cindy observed the sickening stares it became apparent that she was reliving her sister's eighth grade nightmare.

"Girls on this side, boys on that side," Mr. Sermons ordered when they approached the bathhouse. "When you come out we'll meet at the large pool," he said, pointing to the gigantic one with the billowing blue water.

After changing into swimsuits, Hobbstown headed towards the big pool. A few of their classmates from Bradley Gardens sat on the grass with some other white children unfamiliar to

Hobbstown. Hobbstown joined them on the grass.

"Let's go to the other swimming pool," Cindy heard the blonde-haired girl with a lengthy ponytail tell the redheaded girl sitting beside her.

"Why?" the redhead asked. She got up and stuck her foot gingerly in the water. "I like this pool. You said you wanted to swim in the big pool."

Cindy saw the redhead's face turn crimson as it dawned on her why her friend did not want to get in the water. The long-haired girl's friend and most of the other white kids who did not know them joined the two girls as they walked away.

Why did I come here? Cindy fumed. But then said to no one in particular, "We have just as much right to be here as anyone else. I'm getting in the pool." She glanced at Mr. Sermons who stood on the sidelines. She could tell he was taking everything in, as if he had been waiting for them to make the decision for themselves.

"Last one in is a rotten egg," somebody yelled, and before long all of the Hobbstown kids were in the water, laughing and splashing each other. But even in the water they remained at one end of the pool while most of the white children stayed in another area of the water. After getting out of the pool, Cindy noticed they weren't far from the disc jockey.

"Wow, look at that huge tree," Little Henry yelled. He was a first cousin to the Murdock's. His mother Molly Bell and Anna Murdock were sisters. The Bell family was large, and they lived in a ranch on Sussex Avenue in back of the Williams' household. The Bell boys, Henry and Harry, were regularly at the Williams' back door; sometimes they would grab a bite to eat, or just hang with the boys.

She followed his gaze to the gigantic oak with the long willowy branches. The branches seemed to stretch clear to heaven. It drew the Hobbstown children like a magnet, and with the music playing nearby, Cindy nearly forgot that they were a novelty to many in the park.

"I wonder if he has the 'Stroll'?" Cheryl asked.

Yeah, Cindy thought, *because we sure can't Stroll to "Kookie, Kookie, Lend Me Your Comb," or "Lipstick on Your Collar."*

"Ladies and gentlemen, the DJ is now taking requests," a voice came over the microphone.

"Do you have the 'Stroll'?" someone from Hobbstown asked.

The DJ smiled and nodded his head. In a minute the song came on. *This is the sugar we need for our souls,* Cindy thought. Lorraine Grey was the one who called out moves for dancing in lines, but everybody tried to match the rhythm of Cheryl Murdock and Little Henry. They were great dancers. Little Henry mesmerized everyone when he sometimes imitated singer James Brown's moves.

"Three lines," Lorraine said.

Cindy fell in with the rest of the crowd.

"Hit it. Step one, cross right, step back, step three," Lorraine shouted. "And again, step one, cross left, step back, step four." Her long legs flowed to the beat.

"Let's do the Stroll," Hobbstown sang along with the song out of habit, keeping time to the music. As she looked up at the towering tree sheltering them from the sun, Cindy felt the dance come alive just as it did in Hobbstown.

"What dance is that?" she heard the redhead ask the blonde girl who had walked away at poolside. "It looks like fun."

The fair-haired girl kind of stood to the side. She glanced at them and quickly looked away. Nevertheless, a crowd of white children gathered around. They swayed and clapped their hands to the music, as they watched Hobbstown dance smoothly on the soft green grass. Some of the kids from Bradley Gardens joined in and, much to Cindy's surprise, the redhead got right alongside her.

"This is a groovy dance. Can you show me the steps?"

"Sure. Just listen to Lorraine, the girl up front. She calls out all the steps. It's easy."

"Now turn," Lorraine said.

As they turned, Cindy caught sight of the pale ponytail of the redhead's friend as she walked away. She felt sure the redhead would follow her friend, but she didn't.

"I wanna learn this dance," the girl said to Cindy. "I'm Amy," she yelled above the music. They both laughed as she attempted to stay in step.

"I'm Cindy," she shouted back. Suddenly she felt the melancholy cloud of the morning lift and she was having a good time. She only wished her sister Mary Nell could have been there to see that things were changing. *I'll tell her*, she thought. *That will make her happy*. As she looked towards the DJ she saw Mr. Sermons speaking with him. The DJ smiled as he played the "Stroll" again.

Chapter 4

Stewart's Hill

Stewart's Hill was the site of a lofty home situated within an abundance of voluminous trees and greenery on top of a hill bordering Mercer Street. However, today Stewart's Hill can only be found in memories. The assembly of beautiful new homes that grace the hill where the Stewart homestead stood from 1949 to the late 1970s provide no evidence that it existed. After the Stewart's vacated the hill, the Jewett family moved in; however, it continues to be called Stewart's Hill even to this day.

"Let's go up to the mansion to see Ruby and Betty," Cindy heard Gerri Proctor say to her sisters. Gerri lived on Henry Street with her parents, John and Loudia Proctor. She had lots of sisters and brothers; Marian, Sally, Teresa, George (Butch), John, Jr., Kevin, Christopher (Chris), Charles (Chucky), and Vivian. Gerri's comment was met with light laughter, as the girls sat on the Williams' porch winding down after a big Sunday dinner.

"Well, it does remind me of a mansion," she laughed. "Betty and Ruby always dress so sharp and have parties like rich people. I remember when they moved here. They lived in the city before they moved on the Hill in the '50s. You know we're related," Gerri continued. "Their stepmother, Mattie Holloway, is a distant cousin. And George Stewart, their father, is a cousin on Uncle Amos' side of the family.

It was no secret that Willis and Ida Stewart bought the five acres on the hill in 1949 from a white owner for $4,000. The story went that the seller set up a contract for Willis Stewart to pay $300 per month for the first five months and, $500, plus 6% interest on the sixth and final month. Since the typical pay at that time was less than a dollar per hour, and the average black man's wages were less than two thousand a year, it seemed Stewart had been set up for a fall. It was highly unlikely that he could meet the terms. In addition, if any area of the contract was not met, the land and the money paid thus far would revert back to the owner. However, Willis Stewart managed to make all the payments on time, but things got shaky when he could not find the owner to pay the last payment. Mysteriously, the owner had disappeared. Twice, he attempted to find him and pay the final bill. Realizing he would lose everything if the owner did not receive the payment by month's end, he hired a lawyer in Somerville. The lawyer sent the owner the final payment via registered mail, and Willis Stewart became the new owner of the property.

Not too many years later, the Stewart family donated land to Macedonia Baptist Church to build a cesspool so the church could install a bathroom inside the church. Hobbstown had no sewers at that time.

On the few occasions that Cindy visited Stewart's Hill she was captivated by its air of secrecy. It was located on the outskirts of Hobbstown, but was still considered to be in the realm of Hobbstown territory. Massive green trees sur-rounded the property. Peter's Brook ran parallel to the elevated road leading up the hill to the house. In summertime, they picked juicy strawberries from patches tucked away in the rich green grass. Abundant daisies, dandelions, pussy willows, and treasures of four-leaf clover could also be found on the trail. Visiting Stewart's Hill was exciting, and Cindy thought perhaps today her sisters might not mind if she tagged along with them.

"Let's hurry and do the dishes so we can go," Lena said.

So far, Cindy thought, *they didn't say I can't go with them.* On the way to the park she stayed close to her sisters, foregoing her usual walk to Louise or Helen's house. As they strolled on to the Hobbstown park grounds, Cindy noticed that some of her friends were already there. She tried not to appear anxious while her sisters chatted with their friends. Normally she would seek out her buddies in the park, but she didn't intend on staying so she didn't stray. After what seemed an eternity they headed for the two-block walk to Stewart's.

"Come on, Cindy," Mary Nell said. "We can't stay on the hill long since we have school tomorrow."

———

She felt an almost sinful freedom as they swung nearly equal to some of the low trees on the six-person porch swing at the Stewart home. Some of Cindy's friends had made their way to the hill after all, and they pumped the swing wildly. They were high above the ground when the swing appeared ready to buckle. Cindy caught her breath and held on to the chain with all of her strength.

"Higher," Bobby Holloway yelled. DJ was on the swing too. His father, James, one of Reverend Hobbs' sons, married Victoria Rodgers. They raised six children, two of whom Cindy was familiar with, Judy and Betty.

"No, slow down," Lorraine screamed, "before we crash."

Cindy's heart went to her throat as the swing headed full speed backward toward the house. She clutched the chain tighter as it sped, seemingly with a mind of its own, as she turned to look, straight towards the upper window of the Stewart home. Holding her breath, she braced for the impending crash and closed her eyes tightly. Suddenly, miraculously, the swing slowed. As it traveled backward they jumped to the ground in a heap. They laughed uncontrollably now that the hell-bent ride was over.

The air was filled with the smell of tangy barbecue sauce. The kids watched from a distance as George Stewart and his brother Rollin sponged red sauce on the pig. It was split in half and lay on the huge pit located on the side of the house.

George looked over at the crowd assembled on the lawn. "Hotdogs ready," he shouted.

Ruby and Betty Stewart came out of the house with their friends. Their clothes were beautiful and their hair perfectly groomed. Betty's long wavy hair was pulled up in a ponytail with a white bow. The ponytail hung to the middle of her back. She wore an ankle-length blue felt skirt with a stitch of a white poodle just above the hem. Her long-sleeved white cashmere sweater complimented her cream-colored skin. Ruby had on a similar outfit, but her hair fell to her shoulders in a flawless pageboy. They reminded Cindy of the wealthy, sophisticated white girls at school, but in a good way. She watched them mingle effortlessly with their friends, adding a distinct charm to the hill.

Mama had a sister Lauretha, whose daughter, Daisy, lived in Newark with Mama's other sister, Junetta. The children in the family called Aunt Junetta "Anee" (pronounced A-knee). Daisy spent summers with Aunt Mary and Uncle Nearo. She was close in age to their older daughters.

"Ooh, I wouldn't miss Ruby's party for anything," Daisy exclaimed that Saturday evening. Cindy watched the older girls dress for a party on Stewart's Hill. "Aunt Mary said I can have my sweet sixteen party here next year," her words muffled as she pulled the pink cashmere sweater over her head and smoothed it with her hand.

"When did Mama tell you that?" Lena asked.

Daisy shrugged her shoulders, but didn't answer. Lena pulled rollers from her own hair, unleashing curly long locks. As they flitted around the room getting dressed for Ruby Stewart's sixteenth birthday party, Cindy and Diane helped them.

"I wish I could go," Cindy said.

"Your day is coming," Dee said. She wore an ankle-length, black velvet skirt with stitches of red felt cats sewn neatly at the bottom. Her outfit was complete with a matching button-down, red sweater. Each of the girls was dressed in similar skirts with hoop slips underneath and snug-fitting sweaters to the waistline. Mary's sweater was light blue; her skirt was dark blue with light blue poodles. Lena and Daisy wore black pullover sweaters with red skirts. They had come home earlier that day laden with bags from Robert Hall's retail clothing store across Route 22. Cindy hadn't seen their outfits until now, and they all looked beautiful.

"Alright," Mama said, as they walked towards the front door, "be back to the house by midnight. No later."

Daisy batted her lashes at Mama, to whom she bore a striking resemblance. "Alright, Aunt Mary, we'll be home on time," she said. She hugged Mama.

"Okay. Don't let me have to come up on that hill looking for ya'll."

The girls made their way down the driveway to the street. "Ya'll look real nice," Mama said as she smiled.

It was early, just past 7:00 p.m. and still daylight. Cindy read Mama's face to see what her chances might be of walking to the hill and coming right back. Mama looked happy as she waved at Ms. Nonie across the street.

The words tumbled out. "Mama, can I walk to the hill with them and come right back?" Mama's face softened as she looked at her older daughters and then back at her.

"Gone ahead then, and be back before dark."

Cindy squealed with glee and ran to Louise's house. She and Louise stopped to get Helen. When they got to the end of Mercer Street, which led to Stewart's, much of the younger crowd was already at the bottom of the hill. They watched from below as the older teens climbed the hill for the party. They came from all over; Somerville, Plainfield, Manville, Franklin, even as far away as Newark. The best view to the home was from a portion of the road closer to the front of the house. That's where the younger kids gathered. The multi-colored string of lights hanging from the trees cast a dreamlike glow over the sprawling lawn.

"Ooh, look at Ruby," Helen said. "She looks so pretty."

Ruby's dress was pink chiffon. A tiara sparkled on her head in the setting sun.

She looks like a beautiful black Cinderella, Cindy thought.

"Let's sneak up there," Johnny Albert dared. "It's almost dark and if we stay near the back of the house they won't see us." Johnny lived in Somerville but he hung out a lot with the kids in Hobbstown.

It was turning dusk, and Cindy knew she should be getting home, yet her inner voice told her to follow Johnny and the rest of her friends. She watched as he eased towards the house. *Go, stay, go, stay*, ran through her head a thousand times. The allure was too much; she followed the crowd. Her heart beat like a drum as they crept to the back of the house. Nighttime took on new meaning as silhouettes danced on the walls in the house to the sultry melodies from the phonograph. Shadows kissed and held each other close, giving the appearance that they were one. Suddenly the smooth sound of "Smoke Gets in Your Eyes" came to an abrupt end as the "Slop" blasted from the record player. Rhythm-filled teenagers charged from the house to dance in pairs under the tinted lights. Cindy was spellbound as she watched them dance joyfully and their laughter filled the warm night air. "Sixteen Candles" began to play at the same moment she realized the sun was fully set.

"I gotta go," she mumbled to anyone listening, and then took off running down the hill.

"Wait up," she heard a voice behind her. But she didn't stop. She concocted a fib as she darted towards home, rivaling the speed of a track star. Her fear was not from the dark; they had long gotten used to the partial absence of street lights in Hobbstown. Her panic came from the thought that Daddy might get home before her. It was way past dusk when she entered the living room. Her heart pounded all the more when she saw Daddy sitting in the big chair reading his bible.

"Lucinda, way you been this time a night?" he asked hotly, but he didn't get up from the chair. Her heart beat fast, so quickly that she thought it would jump right out of her chest. As the lie rolled off her tongue with such ease she could hardly believe her ears.

"Oh Daddy," she talked fast. "It was terrible. Johnny Albert was riding his bike and got hit by a car." She couldn't believe she had invented such a wild tale. Suddenly she saw her father's distress with her whereabouts fade into thin air. This news about Johnny was more immediate. Shame filled her for lying. Nevertheless, she understood that breaking the house rules brought painful consequences. She had never received a whipping from her father, and she meant to keep it that way.

"Lord, how bad did he get hurt? Is he alright?"

As the heat of deceit moved from her neck to her face, she continued the fiasco: "The car kind of tapped Johnny's bike and he fell off. He cut his arm on the pavement, but he's okay. That's why I didn't make it home until now. I wanted to see if he was alright."

Daddy's gaze went straight to her soul. Mama came into the room and fixed her eyes on her too. After what seemed an eternity, he spoke. "Alright. You hungry?" he asked.

Her father's kindness cut her to the quick with guilt. She had outright lied and seemed to be getting away with it. Yet, the most important thing on her mind was to call Johnny and the rest of her friends so they could back up her story.

"No, Daddy. I'm not hungry. I'm tired though. I think I'll just go to bed." She eagerly exited the living room for the bedroom she shared with Diane and Neallane (Laine). Laine's birth had rounded out the number of siblings to an even ten.

That fall, around the time of Cindy's thirteenth birthday, Carlton and Bell Bergen moved on Stewart's Hill. They were related to the Stewart family. Carlton was fair-skinned, lanky, and exuded confidence. His younger sister Bell was short, stocky, brown in color, and hilariously witty. Carlton became fast friends with the boys in the neighborhood, and Bell was instantly popular because of her jovial personality. But most of all, the younger kids could now spend time at Stewart's Hill without question, since Carlton and Bell were their age.

Pow-Pow. The sound of a firecracker blasted that morning on the bus as it rolled towards Adamsville Elementary School. The girls screamed, while the boys denied lighting it.

"I didn't light no firecracker," Carlton said.

"Don't look at me," Gary Murdock exclaimed. Gary was one of the Murdock siblings. Anna Miller married Andrew Murdock, Jr. and they had nine children: Linda, Gary, Russell, Cheryl, Leslie, Roy, Andrew III, Lydia, and Carolyn.

"Me neither," Bobby Holloway added.

The bus stopped abruptly. Cindy watched with interest as the driver came down the aisle. She could tell he smoldered with anger.

"Who threw that firecracker?" he asked. His question was met with silence.

"Alright then, when we get to the school all of you will go to the principal's office."

"Carlton did it," one of the white girls from Bradley Gardens yelled. Cindy saw the girl's face turned pink as she spoke. She looked frightened.

"You're lying," Carlton shouted. "You didn't see me light no firecracker."

The bus driver's eyes raked over the students and finally settled on Cindy. "Who did it?" he asked.

"I don't know."

His eyes were wide with anger. She quickly looked away. He quizzed the other kids and received the same response from each of them, except for the one girl. She stuck to her story that Carlton lit the firecracker.

"All of you go directly to the principal's office," the bus driver ordered when they arrived at the school. "Bergen," he said, referring to Carlton, "did you set off that firecracker?"

Carlton was tall for his age. He stood almost eye-level with the bus driver. "No, I said I didn't do it. All these other kids on the bus, but you believe one person," he responded.

Hobbstown was marched to the principal's office by the bus driver along with the one white girl. In the principal's office Carlton continued to refute any claim of wrongdoing. As for the rest of the children, they were questioned repeatedly as to, "Who threw the firecracker?" The principal threatened to suspend all of them from school unless someone admitted to the prank.

"I'm not sure who did it," the white girl suddenly cried. Her eyes filled with tears. "But the sound came from where Carlton was sitting. I thought it was him."

Cindy felt no sympathy for the girl as huge tears dripped down her face. Instead, she turned her attention to the principal to see what he would do now. She could tell he was confused because he had no reason to hold them there since no one saw what happened. *Even if someone did see who threw the firecracker,* she thought, *it was obvious they weren't going to tell.*

"All of you go to class," he said. "Your parents will be advised of this incident."

Carlton stood like granite. She held her breath, and prayed he wouldn't say anything to make matters worse. Everyone began filing out of the office.

"So now we can go back to class because the little white girl admitted she don't know who did it, huh?" he asked the principal.

Gee whiz, Cindy thought, *couldn't he leave well enough alone?* Yet she was proud because he was right.

The principal cleared his throat and turned to Carlton. "Go to class, young man," he said, "and stay out of trouble."

Carlton stared at the principal for a moment before he finally walked out of the door. After this incident, Carlton assumed a leadership role of sorts in school, because he stood up to the establishment.

A snake slivered by and just missed her foot. Cindy ran out of the vegetable garden smack into Mama.

"What's wrong?" Mama asked.

"I saw a snake," Cindy answered shakily.

Daddy leaned on his hoe. He wiped sweat from his brow under the big straw hat he wore. It was vegetable harvesting time for Hobbstown families. They grew gardens on whatever property was available next to their homes. In the coming weeks the Williams family would stock the big freezer in their garage full of vegetables, enough to take them through the winter. All of the children worked in the garden.

"Oh, that wasn't nothing but a little garden snake," Daddy assured her.

But nothing could change her mind concerning vegetable picking and planting. She hated it. Insects ran amuck. The sun beat down mercilessly, and before it was over she knew she would be sweaty.

"We got canning and freezing to do," Mama said. "We need to cut these vegetables before the ground gets cold." As Mama meticulously severed a row of corn and it fell into a waiting basket, Cindy knew she could not get out of the task, garden snakes and all.

"Those little garden snakes are out here all the time. They don't bite," her siblings insisted.

It was true, Cindy thought. *None of them had ever gotten bit by a garden snake.* Still, she couldn't shake her dislike for garden work. She looked towards the Bryant house. Reverend Bryant pruned his notorious grapevine slow and precise. It was a sizeable vine and at the height of its season yielded deep purple juicy grapes. Reverend Bryant was generous with the fruits when they were ready to pick. However, unknown to him, sometimes the children didn't wait for picking time.

Mr. Louis and Ms. Mott were in their garden as well, clipping vines and picking vegetables. Sometimes, Cindy didn't know which was worse, working in the garden or collecting eggs from the hen house. Her family had a bad-tempered rooster named "Bob Tail." He chased anyone who came near the hen house, making it almost impossible to gather eggs. She sighed and started up the row, pulling tomatoes off their vines as she walked and placing them in a large bucket.

Chapter 5

More School Days—The Minstrel

During the 1950s and 1960s, public school could be lonely since Hobbstown students were not involved in the social scene. It wasn't that they were not allowed to participate in the social arena within the school, but there was a sense of being unwelcome. While the school system provided exemplary education, for the most part, Hobbstown students missed the collective social interaction that their white peers took for granted.

"Hi, Bonnie," Cindy said, as the two stood at their gym lockers. It was the beginning of seventh grade. Cindy knew Bonnie was upset as she peered at her reflection in the wall mirror.

"Look at my skin," she wailed. "It's so ugly."

As usual, Cindy thought, *Bonnie had put too much liquid foundation on her face.* Her acne problems began in fifth grade. Although she saw a doctor regularly, when the medicine didn't work quickly, a loud outburst of crying was the end result.

"Why don't you try wearing a different makeup?" Cindy asked as gently as she could. She didn't want to hurt her friend's feelings. "Or just put on a little."

"That's easy for you to say," Bonnie replied tartly. "Your skin is smooth and looks pretty."

Cindy shrugged her shoulders, since at school she felt

anything but pretty. The majority of the time she felt like a fish out of water within a sea of white faces. Having Bonnie in gym class had lessened the pain of being picked last for exercises. However, when Bonnie missed school or cut gym, Cindy had come to expect an unpleasant gym period. Ms. Sherbert would say, "Okay, choose a partner." As everyone ran to a friend, many times she was the last to be selected or was left standing alone. However, she was actually fond of Ms. Sherbert because she had a neat sense of humor and treated all the girls the same. At times she changed her selection protocol and had the girls count off in two's or asked them to "team with the person standing next to you." And she noticed that Ms. Sherbert mostly changed the selection process when Bonnie was out.

"We better hurry up," Bonnie's voice cut through Cindy's daydreaming. She saw that Bonnie had already slipped into her gym suit. "That old bag might give us detention if we're late."

She quickly pulled on her blue one-piece gym suit and stuffed her clothes in the locker. "Okay, let's go. But you better get rid of your gum before you get caught."

Bonnie rolled her eyes and spit her gum in the garbage can on the way out. Cindy noticed some of the girls in the in-crowd whispered to each other as Bonnie passed them. They laughed loudly. When she was almost out of earshot, she heard Sally's voice slice through the air as though she wanted her to hear: "That Bonnie is such a slut."

"What's wrong?" Bonnie asked Cindy as they lined up in the gymnasium. "You look upset."

"Oh, nothing."

"Tell me after gym," Bonnie whispered as Ms. Sherbert instructed the class to warm up with sit-ups.

"So, come on," Bonnie said, as the two walked to the cafeteria for lunch. "What did the snobbies have to say today?"

The truth was that Sally and Darla were among the most

popular girls in school. They had their own little uppity group. Cindy had heard them say unpleasant things about Bonnie before, but as far as she was concerned, they really did not know her. Bonnie was a good friend and smart to boot. It always amazed her that Bonnie could cram for a test during study hall and come out with an "A." Cindy was a good student, but not without consistent study.

It bothered her that Doreen had suddenly changed toward them when she became hall monitor that year. Although she said she despised the Sally and Darla crowd, she now behaved just like them. She decided to tell Bonnie what she heard; she deserved to know.

"Sally called you a slut," she blurted out before she could change her mind. "I heard her say it in gym." She fixed her gaze on Bonnie's face, waiting for an angry outburst. However, to her surprise, rather than being upset, Bonnie's sea-green eyes twinkled. She threw her head back and laughed.

"How can you laugh?" Cindy was amazed, thinking of how she had borne her share of problems attempting to fit in at school.

"They're just jealous," Bonnie said, running her fingers through her short, red-brown hair, "because my boyfriend, Bob, is older and smarter than the boys at school. So they can say what they want. Anyway, Sally is no goody two-shoes; she's the slut, and one of these days I'll tell her."

"Hey, ya'll," Bell yelled to them. She stood at the cafeteria entrance. "Where is everybody?" she said as they came closer.

Cindy noticed that the hometown crowd was not sitting at the usual spot by the window. "Well, let's get in line," she said. "They'll be here soon."

Lunch period is the best time of the day, Cindy thought. *Time to connect with Hobbstown friends.* They each paid fifty-cents for lunch that consisted of a hotdog with sauerkraut, french-fries, and a carton of milk. Soon Lorraine, Helen, and Louise slid into seats at the table.

Lorraine looked as though she would burst with a secret as she leaned into the group. "Guess what?" she whispered. "Some girls got caught smoking in the bathroom. It happened right before recess. By the time the teacher came back to class, the bell rang. I was late getting out because she still had to give us homework."

"Ooh, who was it?" they asked, almost in a chorus. Everyone eyed Lorraine.

"Oh, everybody smokes," Bonnie said, mater-of-factly. "But I'm not stupid enough to do it in school."

"Yes, you are," Cindy laughed. "You just haven't got caught." The table trembled with the weight of their laughter. However, the amusement dissipated as quickly as it came when Cindy locked eyes with Doreen who stood at the cash register paying for lunch. Doreen quickly looked away. Darla and Sally were not at the clique table today, so she wondered if Doreen would sit with them.

Bonnie spotted Doreen too, and muttered under her breath, "Look at that little turncoat. She thinks she's hot stuff because she's a hall monitor. I hope she doesn't sit here."

"Well, here she comes," Cindy answered. But with what seemed to be the ease of a summer wind, Doreen swept past them without as much as a "hello." She strolled to the table at the end of the cafeteria where the clique had lunch, and sat down. *Wow*, Cindy thought, *she is really in with them. Darla and Sally aren't even there.*

"I bet it was somebody in that little high-and-mighty group that got caught smoking. And I bet they won't get suspended," Bonnie cracked. "Their parents will take care of it with a phone call to the school."

Cindy glanced at Doreen periodically over their chatter. She appeared lost in conversation with her newfound friends. Since they had been buddies for so long, this new association felt strange. It was clear that Doreen was enjoying a feeling of importance.

R R R I N G. It was time to go to class.

"Hey, did you hear that Annis Ballard won the election for eighth-grade class president?" Joyce Hobbs asked Cindy. They moved through the hallway to their next class.

"Oh really? That's great!"

It was no secret that Annis was one of the smartest students in the school. She was popular with students and teachers alike. But this was really big news since Annis was from Hobbstown.

"Wow!" Cindy was excited. "This means Annis is the first black eighth-grade president in Bridgewater schools."

"Yep."

Annis' election seemed to stimulate Hobbstown's participation in some of the schools extra-curricular activities.

As she walked to the music room at school Cindy's heart pounded with anticipation. It wasn't her desire to become a cheerleader or majorette. She knew well enough that those clubs were out of reach because of color, but since she loved to sing she tried out for the Cross County Chorus. The chorus consisted of about thirty students who performed in concerts at schools across New Jersey. When she approached the door she saw Arla Daniel gazing at a paper taped on the door to the music room. She and Arla were the only black students in glee club that year. Arla turned to Cindy and said, "Well, at least one of us made it."

She swallowed hard because she didn't know exactly what Arla meant. *Well,* she thought, *there's nothing to do except look at the list for myself.* She screamed as she caught sight of her name on the paper; she couldn't believe it. "I made it," she shouted. Then she remembered that Arla didn't make it.

"I'm sorry, Arla. You'll make it next year. Just don't give up."

"Well, they wouldn't let both of us in anyway," Arla said. "So, like I said, I'm glad one of us made it. Lorraine didn't even

123

Annis Ballard

make the cheerleader squad, and everyone knows she's the best."

"Well, one of these days that will change. We just have to keep trying out, that's all."

Arla shrugged her shoulders as if she didn't care, but Cindy knew better. *All of us want to make it into the clubs we try out for*, she thought. In reality, she wasn't surprised that Lorraine hadn't made the cheerleading squad. She knew the unspoken prerequisite to become a cheerleader called for straight hair, light eyes, and even lighter skin.

"See ya later, Arla. Don't forget what I said."

"Yeah, later."

Cindy felt good about impending eighth grade. Her grades were above average and she had made the chorus. Since good grades landed her in a few classes with some of the smart and/ or wealthy students, she eventually became friendly with some of them. Jug happened to be one such person. They had known each other since fourth grade. As she sat in class one day a paper plane whizzed past her head and fell by her shoe.

"Cindy Lou, Cindy Lou," Jug whispered to her back. "Got any jawbreakers?"

She ignored him since Mr. Cunfrie, the English teacher, looked in their direction. Jug was sort of the class clown. He was also smart, popular, and active in the drama club. But sometimes his mischievous nature got the best of him and he became obnoxious, like now. She knew he wouldn't stop until she answered. She waited until Mr. Cunfrie turned to the blackboard.

"Shut up. I don't have any candy today." The quick prick to her back made her jump when Jug poked her with a pencil.

"Miss Williams, please repeat the homework assignment to the class," Mr. Cunfrie ordered.

She felt the heat of ignorance race to her face as an

undercurrent of laughter trickled through the classroom. Thanks to Jug she had not heard the assignment.

"Page 240, Huckleberry Finn," Jug whispered.

"The class is waiting," Mr. Cunfrie warned.

Never had she seen eyes that bulged with such need to humiliate. "The assignment is page 240, Huckleberry Finn," she answered.

Mr. Cunfrie cleared his throat and the sudden light in his eyes dimmed with disappointment. "Class dismissed," he said, right at the bell.

"You jerk," Cindy yelled at Jug as they filed out of class. Jug doubled over with laughter. When he continued to laugh she wanted to do something mean to pay him back. "Just don't speak to me anymore," she said. "You know how Cunfrie likes handing out detention. That was not funny."

"But you gave him the answer, so he looked pretty silly and you looked smart," Jug said.

Her anger began to subside. The truth was that she felt easy with Jug. He was one of the few white students who treated her as if he really liked being her friend. Still, she had to give him a hard time because that was how their relationship went. "If you bother me again like that, I will ask Mr. Cunfrie to move me to another desk."

They reached her locker. She dialed the locker combination, opened the door, and since it was the end of the school day, dumped in the books she didn't need. Jug stood smiling his wide toothy grin. Cindy couldn't be angry with him anymore. He was a thin boy with wispy blond hair and shocking blue eyes. She hadn't noticed until that moment how tall he had grown.

"Make sure you bring me some of Holloway's candy tomorrow," he laughed.

"What, so you can get me in trouble again? You must be crazy. You better go before you miss your bus," she laughed.

"Nope, I have drama tonight. Hey, are you going to the Sock Hop on Friday?" he asked.

Hobbstown usually didn't attend the dances in the school gym unless they planned it in advance. Tomorrow was Thursday and so far everyone said they weren't going.

"No. I won't be going. Why?"

"Just wondering. Okay, see you tomorrow."

"Bye."

It was June 1962. Mary Nell was graduating high school. The family sat in the bleachers waiting for the graduates to appear. Cindy thought of how Daddy proudly mentioned more than a few times that day, that Mary Nell would be "the first 'colored person' to graduate from Bridgewater-West High School in that first class of 1962." It was widely known that Reverend Bryant's daughter, Louise, had been the first African-American from Hobbstown to graduate from Somerville High, but Mary would be the first at Bridgewater-West.

She was proud of her beautiful sister Mary as she stood in line with her classmates. It seemed to take forever for her name to be called. Finally they heard, *Mary Nell Williams.* They clapped loudly as Mary Nell walked to the podium and received her diploma. Yet, that evening back at the house, Cindy noticed that Mary Nell was strangely quiet for such a happy occasion. They were in the bedroom. She watched as Mary promptly pulled off the black graduation robe and hung it far back in the closet.

"Are you glad it's over?" Cindy asked. "No more school."

"You'll never know how glad I am. Just wait until you get there. You'll see what I'm talking about. Even during graduation today it was still the same thing."

"What do you mean?"

"Well," Mary explained, "there really should have been about eight of us from Hobbstown graduating from West today; the first graduating class of Bridgewater-West High. When we left Somerville High after our freshman year and started at West

Mary Nell Williams

in 1959, the others started to dwindle out. Slowly but surely, I was alone. I'm glad I got through it, but I found out today just how prejudiced Ms. Witt is."

"What did she do?" Even as she asked, a familiar chill raced through Cindy's body when she thought of attending the high school.

"Well, Ms. Witt was the teacher appointed to get all the girls in line in the auditorium and help us with our tassels," Mary explained. "After she lined us up, she walked down the line to congratulate each one of us. Of course I was near the end of the line because of our last name. Ms. Witt came down the line, fixing collars and giving each girl a hug and kiss on the cheek. I watched from where I stood. The closer she came the more my stomach turned. It was like I was expecting some sort of slight. When she finally got to me she politely stretched out her hand, gave me a handshake, and said dryly, 'Congratulations.' She didn't even grip my hand, just held it limply, and went as fast as she could to the next girl. When she got past me she started with the hug and kiss again."

"Did you tell Daddy and Mama?" Cindy felt angry. She was more infuriated because deep within she knew nothing would be done.

"There's no sense in that," Mary said.

She didn't argue the point since she knew what her sister said was true. Their parents viewed obtaining a high school diploma right up there with serving God. Daddy and Mama always told them how they had a chance to "make something of themselves." It came to her now how Daddy always said that if they got a decent education they might escape the factory work that his life seemed to hinge upon.

Any racial incidents were more or less viewed as a fact of life, something "you just had to live with and keep going." To their parents, whatever prejudice they experienced at school did not compare to what they or their parents suffered in the south. Cindy knew it wasn't that they were not upset when they went through adversity. She was well aware that it took a lot for her parents to make their lives comfortable, but racial incidents took a back seat. "Just go to school and do the best you can," Daddy would say. And, for the most part, that is what they did. But Cindy swore that day of Mary Nell's graduation that when she got to the high school things would be different. However, first, she had to get through eighth grade.

"Cindy," she heard someone call her name as she walked the hall to homeroom the first day of eighth grade. She turned to see Doreen waving and running towards her. She was puzzled since Doreen had pretty much ignored her during the latter half of seventh grade. As Doreen came closer, she was struck at how bone thin she looked. And her dark brown hair was styled in a flip instead of her usual pageboy.

"Hi, how was your summer?" she asked breathlessly.

This is very strange, Cindy thought. Doreen smiled and talked to her just as she had before becoming chummy with the clique.

"I found out we have homeroom together," Doreen laughed. But Doreen's sudden change of heart left Cindy cold. She behaved like her old friend, but she never explained why she stopped speaking. She had to know.

"What did I do to you that you stopped talking?" she asked. Doreen looked evasive, but not startled. As a matter of fact, she seemed relieved.

"Let's get to homeroom. We don't want to be late on the first day of school," Doreen said. "We'll talk after class." She turned away quickly, but not before Cindy saw the wet mist in her eyes. *What is going on with her?* she wondered.

They walked the short distance to class together, greeting classmates as they rushed to make the bell. But after homeroom she didn't wait for Doreen. She was confused. So, instead, she rushed out of the door intent on getting lost in the mass of students that thronged the hallway.

She walked swiftly down the hallway searching the crowd in a frantic effort to find Bonnie. She finally spotted her near the girl's room going into her locker.

"Bonnie," she screamed. Bonnie flew from her locker to meet her. They hugged. "Look at your hair," Cindy exclaimed. "You dyed it blonde. Turn around, let me see." It was teased high and tapered to her neck.

"Look at you, skinny, did you stop eating altogether?" Bonnie laughed. "Oh, I know, you are so in love that you can't eat."

"Get out. You're the one with the boyfriend. Hey, talk about skinny. Did you see Doreen yet? She is so thin, and boy was she weird when I saw her this morning."

Bonnie shrugged her shoulders. "No. I didn't see her, and I hope I'm not in any classes with her. Well, what did she have to say? I don't know why you even bother speaking to her. The snobs probably don't want to hang out with her anymore. So now she wants to talk to you."

"Yep, she wants to be friends again. We're in homeroom together and math class. I don't know what to do."

Bonnie rolled her eyes. "Well, you can be friends with her again, but I can't. She never really liked me much anyway. She just put up with me because you and I are friends."

"She looks sad."

"So what," Bonnie said. "If Darla and Sally start talking to her again she'll ditch us just like before. I'm not gonna…"

"Hey, what's happening?" Doreen asked. She caught them off guard in the hallway. "Cindy, you left class so fast I didn't get a chance to talk to you."

"I wanted to see Bonnie before the next class."

"I gotta go," Bonnie said. "Don't want to be late for my next class."

"Yeah, me neither. I have chorus. See you guys later," Cindy said. She ran down the hall to the music room, and tried not to think about the hurt look on Doreen's face.

———

As they entered the school gym, Cindy felt nervous. The fall Sock Hop was taking place. She, Lorraine, Helen, Louise, and Joyce Gould made their way to the bleachers. She waved at Jug who was dancing with a small group of students.

"Come on over," he shouted above the music, but they went to the bleachers and sat down. They sat a stone's throw from Darla's little cluster.

"What time is it?" she asked Lorraine, who sat next to her.

"We just got here. Don't tell me you're ready to leave?"

"No..."

Some of the Hobbstown boys walked in and joined them in the bleachers.

"What's hap'nin?" Carlton asked.

"We just got here. Nothing much is going on," Louise spoke up.

"Hey," Carlton sounded happy, "well let's get on the floor and dance. You know?"

"Yeah, we didn't come here to be wallflowers," Bobby chimed in.

Lorraine headed down the bleachers even before they finished speaking. The rest of the group followed. Laughter echoed off the bleachers as everyone danced the pony. When they played the "Locomotion" they all danced in a line. Cindy spotted Jug in the line and noticed he was out of step along with some of the other kids. She could tell from Lorraine's face that she was about to make a crack about the out of sync lines like she did at home.

"Hey," she yelled, but abruptly stopped, and Cindy knew why. They could tease each other in Hobbstown like that, but this was not their territory.

———

Smoke and hair spray hit her in the face as she entered the girls' room. The Sally crowd was there.

"Hi," Cindy said.

"You look nice," Sally said, and she smiled.

At the same time she saw Sally's eyes rake over her pink cashmere sweater and skirt. *Thank God for my older sisters*, she thought. They dressed her well for occasions like this. Cindy observed Sally as she sprayed her hair from the can as if she would never have the chance to do it again.

"Thanks," Cindy said as a wave of hair spray caught her in the throat and she coughed.

"Pretty sweater," Darla said.

"Thanks." She slipped into the nearest stall.

"What's going on in here, ladies?"

Cindy froze as she heard Ms. Dickson's shrill voice. "Who's been smoking? Answer me right now," she demanded.

"No one was smoking," Sally responded. "We were spraying our hair."

"Nonsense, don't lie to me, young lady. I know the smell of smoke. Who's in the stall?"

Cindy's heart fell to her feet. "It's me, Ms. Dickson," she said. "Cindy Williams."

"Well, were you smoking young lady?"

"No. I just came in here a few minutes ago to use the restroom." She hurried out of the toilet and went to the sink to wash her hands. Ms. Dickson's eyes fixed firmly on her and she could tell the teacher thought she was lying.

"I wasn't smoking, Ms. Dickson. Honest."

"That will be all, young lady," she snapped. "Apparently someone was."

Sally looked nervous, but her next words baffled Cindy. "Ms. Dickson, Cindy just came in here, and none of us were smoking. Honestly, there were other girls in here right before us."

Cindy wondered if she was telling the truth because the air had been thick with the smell of smoke when she entered the bathroom. She was surprised that Sally came to her defense since they weren't friends.

Ms. Dickson rolled her eyes and stamped her foot. "Let's go, girls," she yelled. "I've a good mind to report this to the principal's office. Don't let me see any of you back in the girls' room tonight." She held the door open as she continued to speak. "If you do, I'll see you in the principal's office on Monday and you can count on a suspension."

———

"Be glad you didn't go to the girls' room with me," Cindy said to Louise. "Sally and her friends were in there smoking and Ms. Dickson came in."

"Did they get caught?"

"No, but it was smoky. She accused all of us. Sally told her that I had just come in and some other girls had just left. That none of us were smoking. It was strange."

"Sally took up for you?" Lorraine overheard their conversation. "Wow, you must be getting in with the in-crowd," she laughed.

"Oh, right. That will be the day."

———

On the day of the eighth-grade assembly Cindy felt a lethal tension of sorts running through the school. In the week leading up to the event, rumors had spread that the drama club would be performing a minstrel during the assembly. Hobbstown students discussed it, and collectively agreed that if a minstrel took place they would walk out of the auditorium.

Carlton sat in the last seat at the end of a row at the assembly. Cindy could tell he was troubled. She and Bonnie scurried to the next row and grabbed seats close to some of the other students from Hobbstown. Her stomach did flip-flops as shades of that first trip to Forest Lodge hung thick in the air. Soon, the room turned dark except for the stage. The red theater curtains rose to a bouncy musical number. Four male soft-shoe dancers emerged from the left and right sides of the stage. They met in the center and continued their soft-shoe jamboree. Dressed in long-tailed tuxedos of black, with faces painted the color of midnight, their eyes and lips were dipped in alabaster. Jet-black high-top hats completed each outfit. Although their faces were smothered in black, Cindy cringed in her seat. The darkness could not conceal Jug's features.

"Bonnie, that's Jug," she whispered. Anyone that knew him could not mistake the stormy blue eyes in a face given to peculiar facial expressions. Bonnie didn't answer. But Cindy could tell from the look on her face that her worst fear was true. She felt as if someone had slammed her in the stomach and left her breathless.

"What is he doing?" Bonnie asked. Her face turned crimson.

Cindy felt sick and mesmerized at the same time by what she saw on stage. The dancers' wide smiles appeared even brighter with the contrasting black faces. They danced the soft-shoe minstrel as if they did it daily. She looked around for a clue as to whether Hobbstown would go through with their plan. Suddenly Carlton stood up and walked towards the exit. Some of the other Hobbstown boys were right behind him. She hadn't told Bonnie about their plan, and she ignored the question in her eyes as she stood up to leave.

"I'll see you in fifth period," Bonnie said softly. Her words sounded as hollow as the hole in Cindy's heart.

Although she didn't look back, she knew the rest of Hobbstown wasn't far behind because of the curious stares on the faces of the white students. In the hallway everyone stood around wondering what to do.

"This time they won't have to tell us to go to the principal's office," Carlton said. "If we go to our next class we'll be called out anyway to go see the principal since we walked out. So we might as well go to his office now on our own."

"Yeah, let's do that," everyone chimed in.

They walked towards the principal's office. But he came running down the hall and overtook them at the door. It came to Cindy that just as Bonnie's face had been scarlet, the principal's face was flushed as beefy-red as the tomatoes in their garden.

"What's the meaning of walking out of assembly?" he asked.

However, with his question, the floodgates opened and everyone talked at once. As she looked at the principal's face, Cindy was amazed that he truly looked puzzled.

"Sir, the school puts on a minstrel, and we're expected to sit through it?" Carlton questioned.

"It was an insult to us," Cindy spoke up although she trembled inside. She knew she would be in serious trouble at home if she got detention or, worse yet, suspended from school. But something rebelled in her that day and, as much as she did not want to disappoint her parents, she refused to back down.

"I'm not going back to the assembly," she said firmly.

"Me neither," others chimed in.

The principal loudly cleared his throat while opening the door to his office. "Step in, all of you. Tell me what this is all about."

"It's about the school putting on a minstrel and not thinking about our feelings," Carlton said. "Dancing and making fun of us right to our faces. They must be crazy if they thought we would sit there and watch that."

He actually looks embarrassed, Cindy thought as she looked at the principal's face. *As if he really had no idea that the minstrel would have been offensive to anyone.* Her perception of him was that he wasn't a mean man. However, he had never gone out of his way to become acquainted with the students from Hobbstown. He was cordial, but distant. And right now she could tell he was extremely uncomfortable. He was a tall broad-shouldered man. His salt-and-pepper hair was thinning, and wire-rimmed glasses straddled his nose. He stared at them as if he were seeing them clearly for the first time. It was obvious that something they said struck a nerve because he wearily sat down at his desk. He took off his glasses. His fingers trembled as he laid the glasses on the desk.

"Well, the drama show should end shortly, if it isn't already over," he said. "You each have my permission to go to your next class. You're excused from the remainder of the assembly."

That was it? Cindy was stunned. *No apology, no explanation of why they had done it? Just that we won't be punished for walking out of the auditorium?*

As they filed out of the principal's office she felt angry and deceived. She spoke to no one, nor did she look into any of the other students' faces on her way to fifth period math. Instead, she quietly slid into her seat and pulled out her math book. She knew Hobbstown was the talk of the school. As she took out her number two pencil, she felt Bonnie's eyes on her, but she ignored her. She had had it with phony white people.

"So what did I do except be your friend?" Bonnie whispered. "Some people are just ignorant. I'm sorry, Cin. But you know I'm not like that."

She's right, Cindy thought. *Bonnie has always been my friend. It's wrong to take my feelings out on her.* "I'm not angry with you, Bonnie." But she was irritated with herself for the tears that came to her eyes. She swallowed hard to force them back. *They will not see me cry,* she thought. "We'll talk after class."

"Okay."

On her way to Home Economics class she spotted Jug coming down the hall with some other students. Although they had two classes together, she decided that she would avoid him at every circumstance. He stared. She quickly turned away.

"Hi, Cindy Lou," he said. His voice sounded forced and loud.

She did not respond. *Does he really think we could still be friends after what he did?* she thought. She wanted to hurt him like he hurt her. "You're saying hello to me, when you made fun of me today in the worst possible way?"

He looked wounded, and she was glad.

"It was just part of the drama show. It was nothing against you or anyone else," Jug exclaimed.

"I thought you were better than that. But you're a fake, so

please don't pretend that you are any different. You were in blackface and you loved it."

Good, he looks embarrassed, she thought, as his friends backed away. His blue eyes appeared to cloud momentarily. Their eyes met, and in that instant she realized how confident he was in his whiteness. It told her that he could not say he was sorry. When all was said and done he was too proud. But in this they were equals because she was becoming fiercely connected to her heritage. In that moment, the question mark in his eyes measured their friendship. *No, he could not say he was sorry,* she thought. And in her eyes their friendship was over.

"See you around, Jug."

"Yes. I'll see you around."

In Hobbstown, Cindy's friends were a tight-knit group of teens eager to step into the limelight of their youth. They discussed the civil rights struggles going on in the South. Martin Luther King, Jr.'s non-violent approach for equal rights was always at the forefront of their talk, as well as Malcolm X. Cindy was mesmerized with the huge Afro hairdos that many blacks in the South wore. And as she watched the sit-ins and boycotts on television, that feeling of both anger and sadness experienced when the minstrel took place came over her once again.

One day as she, Helen, Louise, and Joyce Gould walked to Holloway's for candy, Cindy said, "I think I'll start wearing an Afro."

She laughed when Louise stared at her as though she had lost her mind. "You're gonna wear your hair to school like that?" she asked.

She really hadn't thought about that, but now that the question was asked she wasn't going to back down. "Well, yeah, I mean to wear it to school like that. Why not? Let's all do it," she suggested. "It will show our support for what's going on in the South." They looked unsure.

"I don't know," Louise said.

"I'll do it," Helen chimed in.

So during that weekend, many of Hobbstown's younger teen girls washed their hair and donned naturals. Cindy used her brothers' hair picks and pomade to give her hair a nice round look. She was surprised that Mama and Daddy didn't say too much about it, just that, "They must be going through a phase."

On the ride to school the following Monday morning she could tell Carlton was happy. He seemed to be in his own little comfort zone.

"Black power!" he shouted. As they laughed, Cindy noticed some of the white kids looked a little uncomfortable. *Well that's too bad*, she thought. *We don't have to wear our hair straight just to fit in. Why does everything have to be Euro to be accepted?* She felt good; a sudden freedom came when she left the hot comb behind and embraced her kinky hair.

As she took her seat in homeroom that morning, her hairdo was met with inquisitive stares. She felt the teacher's discomfort, because she continued to glance at her while providing information to the class. Doreen sat about three seats to Cindy's right and seemed unable to keep her eyes off of her new hairdo. She attempted to run out right after class, but Doreen pushed her way through the crowd of students to get to her.

"Wow, Cindy, your hair looks different," she said loudly. "What did you do to it?"

"I washed it," she said, just as loudly, and walked away. In the corridor she ran head-on into Jug and some of his friends.

Although time had softened her resentment towards him, this was not the day for any of his wisecracks. He stared, but said nothing. She waited for his response simply because she knew he would have one. She stared at him, waiting, not caring if she was late for class.

"Hi," he said.

She smiled with inward satisfaction as his face turned three shades of red. "Hello," she replied. She almost felt sorry for Jug because he was so uneasy, but then she remembered how she felt the day of the minstrel. He seemed to read her mind and chose his words cautiously.

"Are you still singing with the Cross County Chorus?" he asked.

Well, she thought, *he is learning.* "Yes. Are you still in the drama club?"

Chapter 6

The 287 Scare and High School

Although their parents could not protect them from adversity experienced outside of Hobbstown, the town was their safe haven. It was no surprise, therefore, that the younger generation knew little about plans to eliminate Hobbstown.

It was Easter time in 1962. The Williams' household overflowed with relatives. The traditional night-before cooking was nearly completed as the women finished the trimmings. A sweet cinnamon aroma floated through the house from the sweet potato pies cooling on the dining room table. Cousin Annie Jay sat on the living room couch. She always had fun stories to tell that would have the whole family in stitches. Grandma Fennie was at the stove stewing fish in cornmeal and onions. Grandma Fennie, Cousin Annie Jay and Mama loved to fish. They were fishing buddies with Ms. Nonie, and on occasion Ms. Mott.

Cindy sneezed. The strong aroma of the onions she chopped for Mama to finish the turkey stuffing brought tears to her eyes.

"Open your mouth, chil'," Grandma Fennie said to her. She opened her mouth not knowing what to expect. To her surprise, Grandma Fennie stuck a large piece of white bread into her mouth. "Just hold it between your teeth like that. The bread will catch that strong odor from the onions and stop you from sneezin'."

She stared inquisitively at Grandma Fennie, but continued to slice the onions and, sure enough, she ceased sneezing.

"Nell, ain't no truth to that highway thing coming through here is it?" Grandma Fennie asked Daddy.

He sat at the kitchen table drinking coffee as he read the newspaper. From the corner of her eye, Cindy saw Daddy drop the paper and shake his head back and forth. It was as though he didn't want to talk about the question Grandma Fennie asked. Although she was curious, Cindy busied herself cutting up the onions. She knew better than to get into grown folks' conversations.

"Naw, that's just some talk," Daddy said, but Cindy noticed he looked around the room as if he was worried that someone had heard the question. But everyone seemed caught up in cooking chores and didn't seem to have heard. Daddy went back to reading the paper.

She handed Mama the bowl of chopped onions. Mama dumped them in the sink with the rest of the ingredients where she made a huge batch of turkey dressing.

"Aw ain't nothin' to that talk Mama," she said to Grandma Fennie. "It's gonna be fine."

———

"Aunt Mary! Uncle Nell!" Daisy screamed.

Daisy ran into the house, breaking the uncomfortable silence that had suddenly settled in the kitchen.

"Did you see my picture on the magazine cover? Did Anee show ya'll?"

Cindy smiled because she knew Daisy wanted to be anything but a small town girl. She always talked big dreams…searching for that big break that would take her out of the city. Today Daisy had her hair pulled up in a ponytail that fell to her shoulders and she did look glamorous.

Anee laughed and pulled some papers out of her big brown

pocketbook. "Oh goodness, it slipped my mind," she said. She placed the magazine on the dining room table, and everyone gathered around it. The publication was *Bronze Thrills*. Cindy had seen it many times before. It was a romance magazine much like *True Story* publication. However, the stories in *Bronze Thrills* were about black people, and there was always a beautiful model on the cover.

Daisy a model? She wondered if it were true. But finally the magazine was passed to her, and much to her surprise, Daisy was on the cover as big as day, just like she said. *She looks beautiful*, Cindy thought, *like an exotic model from the Caribbean.* "Our cover model, Sophia, is from Bombay, India, an aspiring actress," the caption read. She could tell Daisy loved the attention. *Who could blame her*, Cindy thought. *This was the biggest thing that anyone they knew had ever done.*

Daddy picked up the magazine and stared at the picture. He smiled and kind of chuckled. "Well, I declare," he said. "Me-me, that's you ain't it?" Me-me was Daisy's family nickname. "Yeah, it sho' is," Daddy answered his own question. "Umph, umph, umph. Well ain't that something?"

"Yes, Uncle Nell, that's me," Daisy said.

Although he smiled, Daddy's eyes looked troubled, but not about the picture. It was something else. However, her worry was soon overtaken by the coziness of family fun and talk late into the evening. All the adults sat around the dining-room table chatting after the cooking was complete, while the kids mingled in the living room.

"Ya'll children come on over to the house. I'm gone make some ice cream," Aunt Nolia said. Aunt Nolia hand-cranked rock salt and cream with vanilla flavor a few times during the summer in her garage ever since Cindy could remember. The ice cream was as smooth as silk, and Aunt Nolia said it was because of the number of churns. It was scrumptious, and the only complaint was that Aunt Nolia didn't make it often enough.

"I don't know, Nolie. It's still pretty cool out," Daddy said.

Aunt Nolia laughed her hoarse, raspy whisper. Then she drew deeply on her Camel cigarette and blew the smoke out in a billowy stream. "Aw, Nearo, the ground been thawed from the winter. A little cold air won't hurt these children. It's good for 'em. It don't make no sense to sit around and worry about that highway talk anyway...they can't make nobody move away from here."

Move away from Hobbstown? Why? Cindy wondered. She knew at least some of her siblings heard Aunt Nolia, but they didn't appear to be particularly alarmed. A nervous glance passed between Daddy and Mama. Daddy jumped up from his seat. It reminded her of his reaction when he received a call to do a plumbing job, swift and direct.

"Yeah, well I guess it a be alright then. Gone ahead," he said.

It was easy to see that he did not want Aunt Nolia to keep talking about the highway thing, whatever it meant.

"Ya'll put ya hats and gloves on," Mama said. "This the time of year to get sick. And come on back to the house when ya'll finish the ice cream."

Pow, pow, came the sound of a car backfiring in the same moment Bell puffed her cheeks, crossed her eyes, and blew out the candles on her birthday cake.

"What was that?" everyone yelled. They ran to the front door. A white man was backing up a big brown car in the driveway.

"He probably got turned around," Carlton said. But to everyone's surprise, the man didn't pull off, instead he cut the engine. He sat in the car squinting and using his hand as a shield from the summer sun glare. The man gazed at the house and stretched his neck as if to see as much as he could of the area. Although he glanced at them as they stood watching him, it was clear that they were not the object of his scrutiny.

Mr. Bergen pulled into the driveway, and the man then

started his car. No one said anything, but there was a sense of relief in the air. Of course, there were familiar merchants who brought their wares to Hobbstown to sell. To name a few, the Dugan man brought bread and baked goods on his brown delivery truck. There was also a daily milkman. Franks regularly delivered soda and candy to the Holloway's. And the Town Shop tailor came on a regular basis to fit some of the men with tailor-made suits. Hobbstown was accustomed to seeing these merchants, but this man was unfamiliar.

Some of their mothers took in ironing or did days' work for white folk in the area. It was no surprise to see them drop off and pick up clothing or transport the women to and from their homes. However, there was an air of uncertainty since there was no specific reason for the gentleman to be there.

"Can I help you, sir?" Mr. Bergen asked the man.

It was easy to see the stranger was caught off guard. "No, I just didn't realize how much land was up here," he said. "I've never been through here, although I live in Bridgewater. Sorry to bother you." Suddenly, he seemed to be in a great hurry and began pulling out of the driveway.

Mr. Bergen stood quietly as the man drove down the hill. He then turned towards the house. "They up to something," he said to nobody in particular.

Cindy saw that he wore the same look of concern as Daddy and Mama on Easter Sunday.

———

"How ya'll girls doing?" Mrs. Holloway asked as Louise, Helen, and Cindy chose penny candy from the boxes full of Tootsie Rolls, Hot Balls, Sugar Daddies, and bubble gum stationed neatly on the counter.

"We're fine."

"Got plenty of red hots, too," Mrs. Holloway said. "Just getting ready to open them up and put them out on the table."

Cindy was happy because between the three of them they

had collected nine empty soda bottles. Mrs. Holloway gave two cents for each bottle returned. That meant they each got six cents for the bottles. She had some other change, so that would give her an even twenty cents to spend.

"Ella, I'm going next door to the church to that meeting 'bout 287 coming through here," Mr. Holloway said as he entered into the room. "Oh. Hello, girls. I didn't realize nobody else was down here."

He smiled at them, and his gold tooth twinkled like a light as sunbeams caught it through the open window. Mr. Holloway continued to talk about the highway. "Well, we'll find out the truth now about this thing," he looked at his wife.

"I'm just talking to the Lord about it," Mrs. Holloway said, "and He done told me everything will be alright." Mrs. Holloway was a big woman, light-skinned with wavy, black hair that hung to her shoulders. Cindy was fond of her, as all the children were. She was a nice lady, warm, caring, and easy to talk to. But right now, she could tell Mr. Holloway didn't altogether believe what Mrs. Holloway said. He shook his head back and forth.

"Well, you right about one thing, it will work for us or against us, but we can't just sit and wait. These are our homes they talking about taking. We didn't come all the way up here from south for all these years to lose our property."

That kind of talk made Cindy anxious. She was surprised the conversation didn't seem to affect her friends. But she decided they were busy picking candy so perhaps they hadn't heard. She finished selecting her candy. "Can I get a Coca-Cola, too?" she asked Mrs. Holloway.

"You sure can, darling." She pulled a bottle of soda out of the ice box.

Cindy paid her fifteen cents for everything and waited for Helen and Louise to finish. She was on edge now and anxious to leave. A flood of half conversations overheard at the homes of friends in Hobbstown came to mind. Bits and pieces like "they got a plan," "they up to something," and "287 coming" clamped around her heart like icy fingers. She remembered how the words resonated from house-to-house like a tight rubber ball.

"Ya'll take care, girls," Mrs. Holloway said. The three of them walked up the stairs from the store basement into the cool of the day.

———

As she walked the outside corridor of Bridgewater-West High School in 1963 as a freshman, Cindy marveled at the beautiful flowers growing on each side of the long outdoor walkway. Compared to Adamsville Junior High, the school was gigantic.

She almost didn't recognize Doreen in a long black leather coat as she came towards her. "Hi Cindy," she said. She sounded different, tough. And Cindy noticed she was with Macy and Ginger, who were definitely not part of the Sally and Darla crowd. In addition, Doreen wore a ton of makeup and her usual pageboy hairdo was teased up to the sky. She was puzzled because Doreen would not have given Macy and Ginger the time of day in junior high. As far back as Cindy could remember the two girls were troublemakers. However, it had come as no surprise when the Darla crowd showed Doreen their true colors and she found herself no longer in their good graces.

"Hey, what's happening?" Cindy asked, attempting to hide her surprise at Doreen's appearance, and the fact that Doreen spoke to her. They had parted ways some time ago.

"You know Macy and Ginger don't you?" Doreen asked.

Who didn't know them? Cindy thought, but said, "Sure, hi."

"This school is groovy," Doreen said. "We're going to have a blast in high school."

"Yeah, real cool," Macy acknowledged. Ginger just smiled.

"It's huge, lots of buildings to get used to," Cindy said, "but it's pretty."

"Okay, we'll dig you later," Doreen said.

This new trying-to-be-hip Doreen just didn't fit and Cindy laughed. But when she saw the look of anger on Doreen's face she wished she could take it back.

"So, what's funny?" Doreen asked. The three girls surrounded her.

"Oh, nothing," Cindy said lightly. Doreen's gaze appeared threatening. Cindy wondered why she had changed so and why she had suddenly become the object of her discontent. She certainly wasn't afraid of Doreen or her friends, and she pushed through their circle to let them know it. "See ya later," she said, and walked to her first class in the 400 building.

———

Bonnie and Cindy realized at the end of eighth grade that they had only one class together that year, math. However, they did have the same lunch period. Bonnie's green eyes were wide with interest at the lunch table after Cindy reiterated the encounter of that morning with Doreen and her new friends.

"If you ask me, she's on pot or something," Bonnie said, snapping open a bag of chips. "She's the one that stopped talking to us after she got with those other girls. They dumped her cold after they found out what a nut case she is."

"Um, well, I guess I wasn't too nice to her last year when she tried to be friends again. I just don't want to be bothered because you never know where she's coming from…you know, Bon?"

"Yeah, she's so two-faced. I saw her strolling the hall in the 300 building this morning like she owned it. Ginger and Macy walked with her like she's a queen bee or something. They had on black leather coats. Macy and Ginger will probably end up kicking Doreen's butt before it's over," Bonnie laughed.

Still, something told Cindy that this wasn't the last of Doreen's bizarre behavior. "I swear, it seems like she will do anything to be popular," she said, "and she is because in every class so far she is the main topic. During English I overheard

Sally talking about her. 'She is such a loony-tune,' she said. 'Remember the movie *Three Faces of Eve,* that's Doreen.' Then they laughed like crazy."

Bonnie picked up the other half of Cindy's tuna sandwich and took a bite before she responded. "Serves her right. Did she really think that snotty little group would be her friends for real? I mean, come on, some of those kids get dropped off to school in limos, and their families are like, wow, so rich. Doreen must have forgotten where she came from. Anyway, she's all talk. We've known that since grade school."

"Yeah, you're right. This is just a passing fancy knowing Doreen. Let's hope it's a quick one."

"It will be. You'll see."

———

At home, the cat was out of the bag. It seemed imminent that Hobbstown was going to be destroyed. Rumors swirled, and it felt as if a dark cloud of fear and distrust hung over the town waiting to whisk them away. These days she noticed that Daddy's face was riddled with concern, though he didn't talk about it. He worked day and night and from bits of conversations that he and Mama had, she gathered they were saving all they could in case the highway thing did happen.

However, everyone else in and outside the family now spared no words regarding the 287 threats to Hobbstown. There was another Williams family living in Hobbstown. Jerry Williams married Claude Miller's daughter, Mary, and they had a large family as well. He was heavily involved in the movement against the highway. They lived in the house that belonged to Babe Miller.

Cindy visited Joyce Hobbs one Saturday afternoon. After Joyce finished her chores the two walked towards the park.

"Let's stop at Uncle Amos' house for a minute," Joyce said as they walked up Henry Street. "Maybe he'll give me some money," she laughed.

They walked in Reverend Hobbs' door to find the front room filled with people, mostly men from the town. Joyce's great-uncle and his guests were in a heated debate about highway 287.

"Naw, we got to do more than just talk amongst ourselves about this," one of the men said. "They mean to level all these homes back here so 287 can take a straight course."

Mr. Williams stood up and kind of walked back and forth before he spoke. "I say we demand a meeting with the Bridgewater Township Board. This is a time when we really have to band together. They talk about this 'eminent domain' thing, but we got families to worry about. What about that? I say we fight until the bitter end. All the backbreaking work we've done in this town and now they say they need our land for a highway? I say they have other options," he said, and sat back down.

Mr. Holloway leaned forward on the sofa. "Well, it's sho' scheduled to come through Mercer Street. That would level all our homes down here between Mercer, Henry, and part of Sussex. The church would be gone, including Stewart's property on the hill. I'm with you, Williams. Let's get a meeting with the Municipal. We done met with one another many a time, at the church and so forth, but let's get the folks that count in a meeting to hear our side."

"Yeah, let's do that," some of the others chimed in.

Reverend Hobbs hadn't noticed the girls standing at the door until then. "Come on in, chil'ren," he said, beckoning to them.

Joyce hugged him.

"How ya mama and daddy doing?" he asked Cindy.

"Oh they're fine, Reverend Hobbs."

"That's good. That's real good." He reached in his pocket and pulled out a dollar bill and handed it to Joyce. "Now make sure you share it with your friend," he said.

"Thanks, Uncle."

The makeup of the Williams' home was changing. Some of the older children graduated high school and now had full-time jobs. George enlisted in the Air Force. Mama's young cousin, Arscko Raines, graduated high school in Sneads, Florida, and came north to live with them. He landed a job at Art Colors, where many area blacks found employment. Soon, he bought a beautiful white Bonneville convertible with red interior. That summer Lit bought a shiny metallic green GTO stick-shift. Although it wasn't brand new he spruced it up with magnum wheels, and it was one of the sharpest cars in town. Some of the other young men in Hobbstown bought popular older model cars of the day, Chevrolets and Fords. Sunday was the day the Hobbstown park usually teemed with cars, as they tinkered under the hoods of the vehicles.

Despite the fact that Cindy could not drive, obtaining a job and buying a car became a priority. But she knew she needed a real job. As soon as school was out she applied for and obtained a full-time summer job at the Holland-Rantos packing plant in Bound Brook.

Lena was teaching Cindy to drive on Mama's old "Betsy" car. The back road, Sussex Avenue, was still mostly dirt. A few evenings a week Lena would take her out to practice. Up and down the road they went, leaving a dusty trail in their wake.

One day as Cindy drove slowly down Sussex Avenue, Lena suddenly screamed, "Get over! Get off the road!" she screamed.

Car engines revved. They were so loud it seemed the car would bear down on them. *ZOOM, ZOOM, ZOOM.* Cindy checked the rearview mirror and quickly turned the car into Adam's Lane. Her heart thumped out of control as a speeding car narrowly missed their tail end.

"They're playing that dog-gone 'chicken,'" Lena said. Her eyes followed the car. The back road billowed with dirt clouds. As it flew by, another car simultaneously streaked down Monmouth Avenue and was soon out of sight.

Errch, errch! The sound came from the end of the two streets as the speeding cars came to jerky stops. They then turned around and raced back up the two streets. Drag-racing was a frequent pastime with the young men of that day. They counted themselves as "blood brothers" and sometimes drag-raced to pass the time away.

Cindy thought of how Ms. Jenkins sometimes cautioned as they played hopscotch or jumped rope in the street. "Ya'll children get out the way! Them boys gone crazy with them cars. I'm praying nobody gets run'd over. Then, too, they can do that out here 'cause the police don't bother to come. I reckon if something did happen though, like a accident, they'd come see 'bout it. What you think, Jenk?"

"Yeah," Mr. Jenkins would say. "Seem mighty strange they might would come when somebody dead, but not before to stop it. Well, I guess that's just how the world done become."

The wind was arctic that day in 1963. Cindy pulled the hood of her car coat over her head and scurried down the breezeway on the way to class in the 600 building. She noticed huddles of students looked forlorn. Some cried. *Something is really wrong,* she thought. *What could have happened?*

As she entered the 600 building a girl screamed, "Oh, my God, they said he was shot."

By the time she made it to class she was a bundle of nerves. Once there, more students wept and the teacher stood wringing her hands. Her eyes looked glassy and red. Cindy sat down in her seat with a profound sense of dread.

"Boys and girls," the teacher began to speak, "today we have lost our President." Suddenly the scratchy PA system came on.

"Quiet," the teacher shushed the class.

"Ladies and gentlemen of Bridgewater-Raritan West High School," came the principal's voice, "it is with great sadness we report that the President of the United States, John Fitzgerald

Kennedy, was shot to death today in Dallas, Texas, at 1:35 p.m."

Cindy sat rooted to her chair in shock. She stared at the clock. It was 2:00 p.m., November 22, 1963.

———

The white students talked of their intentions of attending college after graduation. Cindy also wanted to attend college. She was excited since she chose college prep courses for upcoming tenth grade. She anxiously waited for her chance to speak to Ms. Fats, the guidance counselor. Finally, the day of her appointment with the counselor arrived. Ms. Fats had the schedule in her hand when Cindy entered the office.

"Sit down, Miss Williams," she said. She pushed her cat-eyed glasses back on her nose, and Cindy was happy to see a welcoming smile on her face. She smiled back at the counselor. Her grades were good, and she felt confident that the classes she selected would be approved.

Ms. Fats cleared her throat. "I've studied the courses you have here, and I've recommended some changes. You have nice grades, but I'm not sure if the financial backing needed, academic scholarships and such would come your way."

Cindy's heart sank. In so many words Ms. Fats advised her that even with a small scholarship, her family would not be able to afford the remaining costs of college. She concentrated on holding back the sudden well of tears while Ms. Fats changed her schedule.

"Let's see, general math, English 2, Spanish, general history, science, art, and typing 1," she said. "The typing will be especially good for you. Being a secretary is a good steady job with a decent salary." Ms. Fats stood up, signaling the meeting was over. "I'll submit the schedule for next year."

Cindy swallowed hard as she stood up. She willed herself not to cry in front of this woman who had clipped her wings so impeccably in less than ten minutes. *No wonder so many Hobbstown kids drop out of school,* she thought. *No one here cares about us; whether we get jobs or drop off the face of the earth.*

Later that day, she pretended to be buried in her textbook in English class as Jug walked past her desk to his seat. He had paused at her desk, but then walked on to his seat. *Why won't he just ignore me?* she prayed. Instead, he attempted to behave as if they were still buddies. *He really fooled me good,* she thought. *But he won't get the chance to do it again.*

"Hi, I'm Kate, Kate Peterson," the girl in the seat to her right said.

"Hi, I'm Cindy Williams." She did not recognize Kate from Adamsville School. But there were so many more kids at the high school than in junior high. Etta Douglas, one of Cindy's friends, sat in the seat to her left. The two had known each other since grade school, but got close during eighth grade. "Do you know Etta?" she asked Kate.

Kate leaned over to say hello to Etta and a whisp of blonde hair, which was in a flip, fell into her face. "No. Hi, Etta."

"Let's get started with last night's homework," Ms. Clarefoot said, tapping a ruler on her desk. "Please break into groups of four and study the grammar quiz," she added. "While you are doing that I will check for absences."

The pangs of grade school isolation crawled up Cindy's spine, but Etta and Kate pulled their chairs around her desk. Jug sat a few seats over. *He wouldn't dare join our group,* Cindy thought. She held her breath as he looked their way.

"Hey, Jug, come on over," Etta said. Cindy watched in exasperation as Etta smiled at him with her huge brown eyes.

"We need you over here, Jug," one of the boys mercifully shouted from another section. "Come on over, my man," he insisted. Cindy breathed a sigh of relief when Jug turned to join the boys.

She felt gloomy walking home from the Hobbstown park that evening. Even the beautiful poplar trees that lined Monmouth Avenue on both sides looked melancholy as talk of 287 spiraled out of control. Their branches seemed to sag to the ground as if, like the men and women of Hobbstown, they carried the weight of the world on their shoulders.

When she entered her home she heard Uncle Johnny talking to Daddy in the kitchen. She was struck at how his voice went high and low like a lyrical song. "Well, Nearo, what Hobbs said is the road, if it comes, is gonna mostly affect down the street."

"Johnny, I been talking to the Lord about it. I'm confident in Him that He'll bring us on through. There ain't nothing the Lord can't work out. But we got to trust Him. It's already done."

Usually, whenever Daddy spoke in that manner, Cindy felt that nothing could ever hurt them. But by now she knew the threat of 287 was very real, and as much as she tried not to think about it, she understood that everyone concerned was frightened. The thought of possibly leaving Monmouth Avenue filled her with sadness. Everything appeared dark and threatening and she felt an undeniable bond with the drooping poplar trees.

Although there was a constant chill in the air that perhaps they would lose their homes in the near future, the parents made the best of it. Mama and Daddy still piled their younger children in the car for Friday night trips to Packard's Farmers Market in South Somerville. One Friday night when they returned from the market Reverend Bryant came right over.

"Reverend Bryant, what's going on?" Daddy asked.

Reverend Bryant took his pipe out of his mouth and stood quietly. He seemed to be weighing his words.

"We had that meeting last night with the Board. Things don't look good. They got plans to bring that highway 287 straight through Mercer Street. Right through that back area where the church is, and Holloway's home too. Offered 'em money, but they don't want to pay what they rightly deserve for they homes."

Daddy shook his head. "Ya'll run on, children," he said, and went back to his conversation with Reverend Bryant. "Sho' nuf?" he exclaimed. The children were not quite out of hearing distance. "I tried to make it home in time to go to the meeting, but one of my houses up town had a leak in the basement. I had to go take care of it. By the time me and the boys got back the meeting was over."

"Well, they put up a good fight," Reverend Bryant said. "Jerry Williams, Holloway, Stewart, Miller, Reverend Green, the Hobbs', they all was there. Gave 'em a good argument about how they wouldn't be able to find homes for what they was gone give 'em for these homes out here. Where can they move to with all the children?"

"That's the truth," Daddy responded. "But it's a hard thing with that law that allows the township or government to take property when they looking to build up an area with roads and such."

"Yeah. That's right. They call it 'eminent domain' or something 'nother like that," Reverend Bryant said. "Well, what they said, too, is it might not touch up the street, but ain't no tellin'. When they get done the whole town may be gone."

Kate was out of breath when she caught up with Joyce Hobbs and Cindy in the school hallway. They were changing classes. As she approached them, she blew the ever-present wisp of blonde hair back from her face. She caught Cindy by the arm.

"What happened between you and Doreen?" she whispered.

She wasn't surprised at the question. Lately Doreen did not attempt to hide her anger with her. However, Cindy avoided her and her new friends like the plague. She shrugged her shoulders to show Kate that it didn't matter. "Well, we were friends since grade school, but this year she really changed and got weird with her new friends. I just ignore her. Why? What's going on?"

An abrupt shove caused Cindy to momentarily lose her balance. She broke the fall and turned to see who had pushed her so violently.

Doreen stood there; her eyes looked wild. "So why don't you talk about me to my face?" she asked hotly.

Cindy was still trying to comprehend the reality that Doreen had actually pushed her. *Oh, she must have truly lost her mind,* she thought. Anger blinded her. The only thing that mattered at that moment was to retaliate in the same way.

"Don't get in trouble, Cindy," Kate said. "Let's go to the principal's office. Come on. We'll tell him what happened."

"What is wrong with you, girl?" she screamed at Doreen, ignoring Kate's suggestion. "I wasn't talking about you. And if you touch me again, it's a fight."

"Come on, Cindy, let's go," Joyce said.

"Yeah, I knew you wouldn't fight me. So now you think you're too good because you hang out with the snobs. You laughed at me with Sally and those other snots," Doreen accused her.

"What? Doreen, I don't have time for your nonsense." Cindy turned to go into the girls' room. Doreen followed her into the bathroom.

"Doreen, I'm telling you, you better leave me alone."

"And so what are you going to do if I don't?"

That's it. She grabbed Doreen by the hair with as much force as she could muster. They tussled and fell to the floor as books flew every which way. She held Doreen down with one knee and punched her in the arm. Doreen reached up and yanked her hair. They scuffled into one of the stalls. Suddenly, Doreen fell with her head next to the toilet. Cindy grabbed her by the hair again, determined to stick her head in the bowl.

"Let me go," she yelled as Joyce and Kate held her arms back.

"Do you want to get suspended from school because of her?" Kate screamed.

Cindy stared at Doreen as she attempted to get up from the floor. Tears streamed down her face as she sobbed. The look on Doreen's face filled her with pity and shame. Doreen was sad, but so was she. She didn't dislike Doreen, and now she felt strangely sorry for her. She knew how it felt to be on the outside looking in. For the most part, that had been the story of her life at school.

"I'm sorry, Doreen," she said, and stretched out a hand to help her up. Doreen took it and pulled herself up from the floor.

"Let's get out of here before a teacher comes in," Joyce said.

Kate helped Cindy pick up her books. "C'mon, let's hurry and get to class," she said.

"Nobody likes me," Doreen cried. "Cindy, you were my best friend, but you wouldn't talk to me anymore. Then you started hanging out with THEM. I couldn't believe it."

"No, Doreen. You stopped talking to me, remember?"

"I didn't mean it," Doreen said. "I know what I did wasn't right. I mean not speaking to you and Bonnie after we were friends for so long. I'm sorry."

She does look sorry, Cindy thought. *Always be ready to forgive*, her father's famous words overpowered any further need to settle the score. "Doreen, just because I have a few classes with some of those girls doesn't mean I hang out with them. It's school, and when it's over, so is our friendship. We come from different worlds. Oh, just forget it. I'm leaving."

Suddenly, the door opened and in walked Ms. Fats. "Shouldn't you girls be in class?" she asked. "The last bell rang."

"Doreen wasn't feeling well," Kate said quickly.

Ms. Fats looked under-eyed. "Then she should go to the nurse's office. Doreen, what's the matter?" she asked. As they waited for Doreen's response during the deathlike silence, Cindy held her breath.

"I felt nauseous so I came to the girl's room. I dropped my

books and they were helping me pick them up. I'm okay now. I feel better."

Ms. Fats stared at the girls. She pulled off her cat glasses as if to get a better handle on the situation. Cindy could almost see the wheels of suspicion doing overtime in her head. "I find it hard to believe all these books on the floor belong to you, Doreen. But pick them up and get to class. All of you," she said.

There was a crowd of men standing outside Macedonia Baptist Church that evening as Cindy and Lorraine came from Holloway's empty-handed after finding a sign on their front door that read "CLOSED, OPEN TOMORROW." A shiver ran down Cindy's spine when she noticed a few white men standing in front of the church. Reverend Green was speaking with them. Some of the men of Hobbstown were there, and they did not look happy.

"Oh, tonight is the meeting with the borough. I forgot," Lorraine said.

"Oh, let's go in," Cindy said, and at the same time couldn't believe her own suggestion.

Lorraine's eyes grew big in surprise. "You must be kidding?"

"No, I'm not."

Although fear crawled through her body like a snake, Cindy could not back away from the church if her life depended on it. So, after everyone entered, the two quietly slipped in and stood in the foyer behind the swinging doors. Cindy pushed one door open just a crack and saw the men sitting in pews at the front of the church. She shivered as their voices echoed through the room in the eerie setting. When she glanced at Lorraine, she had one hand over her mouth.

"Well, sir," the Reverend addressed the room, "the township would certainly be placing a tremendous burden on the families of Hobbstown if 287 came through here. It would be devastating."

The room was silent. A sudden cough made her jump as it cut through the stillness.

Jerry Williams spoke up. "The truth is, we have no place to go," he began. "We have large families and the money being offered is not enough to buy property anywhere else. Why should we have to move into apartments and pay rent when we have our own homes here? And most of us couldn't afford the rent for all the rooms we would need. It would be like throwing money out the window."

One of the white men loudly cleared his throat before speaking. "Well, the plans don't include taking all the property of Somerset Manor, just a portion," he said. "You may be able to build homes farther up the street. There's quite a bit of property here, especially on Sussex Avenue."

Mr. Miller rose to his feet. "Now the way I see it is, even if we could build up the street, where are we gonna live in the meantime? Sir, with all due respect, I have seventeen children. I don't believe no one could take in such a big family. The average family living out here has nine or ten children."

"We been through a lot out here building the place up," Reverend Hobbs spoke. "And if the truth be said, we haven't asked the township for nothing much either. Now what we accumulated seem like that's gone be taken away from us. It's the God's honest truth every man out here 'bout broke they back to keep a roof over they family's head. This would be a real tragedy. Like Williams said, 'We got no place to go.'"

"I can't listen anymore," Lorraine said. Her voice sounded shaky, on the verge of tears. Lorraine's family was related to the Miller family. Their house was next door to Mary and Jerry Williams' home.

"C'mon, let's go," Cindy said, as she gently let the door go. "My dad said everything will work out. We just have to wait."

"I'll walk with you as far as Adam's Lane," Lorraine said.

"Okay. We better hurry. It's getting dark."

A few weeks later on a Sunday afternoon, Helen, Louise, and Cindy returned from a walk to the local Dairy Queen. Sometimes they walked in a large group when some of the down-the-street girls joined them; Joyce Gould, Lorraine Grey, and on the way they stopped for Cheryl Murdock. The girls would put on their Sunday best clothes and take the half-mile stroll over North Bridge Street for ice cream. But today, it was just the three of them.

"Are we going to the park later?" Helen asked.

"Yeah," Louise said. "Ya'll come by for me in a little while."

Cindy didn't say anything. She wasn't sure if she would be able to come back out later. Daddy had founded the Traveler's Fellowship Baptist Church in Stelton. The family often went back to church on Sunday evenings for a second service.

"Hey, good-looking," Uncle Johnny greeted Cindy with a pull of her ponytail when she entered the house. He and Daddy sat at the dining room table eating chocolate cake and drinking coffee. It dawned on her that they were unusually gleeful.

"Hey, Unc. Hey, Daddy and Mama," she said.

"Thought you was at the park with the rest of the kids," Daddy said.

She could have kicked herself for coming home. The truth was she thought her siblings had come from the park in case they had to go to church.

"I just came to get some money for Holloway's. I told them I would come back in a few minutes."

"Ya'll come on back to the house. School tomorrow and things got to be straightened out around here," Mama said from the kitchen.

Okay, Cindy thought. *We won't be going back to service.*

"Alright then. Here's a dollar," Daddy said. "Tell the rest of 'em to head on back home now, hear me?"

"Okay. Thanks, Daddy."

"Okay, my little girl," he said.

Before they could change their minds, she made a beeline for the door. She shut it behind her to muffled laughter.

"Lord, these kids sho' nuf growing up," she heard Uncle Johnny exclaim through the door.

'They sho' is. Well, thank the Lord that 287 stuff is over," Daddy commented. Cindy stood still on the steps. "God fixed it so they changed that highway to go past Hobbstown. I tell you the truth, Johnny, I was happy as I don't know what when I heard they gone run it past Woodlawn Avenue."

Cindy jumped down the porch steps and headed for Louise's house feeling happier than she had in months.

1997 Family Wedding—Cindy & Siblings
Front row, left to right: Lena, Cindy, Diane, Dee
Back row, left to right: Nearo, Jr., Litdell, George, Mary
Nell, Neallane, Frank

Chapter 7

The Passionettes—
More School Days, and Death

The parents sought to keep the youngsters enveloped in Hobbstown's gentle cocoon. However, they were destined for change as they transitioned into young adults. Du-wop music had taken hold of Hobbstown, as it had the nation, and in the mid-1960s the Passionettes girl-group was born. But there were hurdles to climb that brought them to the brink of heaven and lows that saw them almost level to the ground.

"Ladies and gentlemen of the Dreamboat Lounge," the master of ceremonies shouted into the mike, "all the way from Hobbstown, New Jersey; give a big hand to the Passionettes!"

Surely they can hear my heart pound even over the thunderous applause, Cindy thought. The four singers ran on stage to a packed house. As always, the hush that saturated the air just before they sang was magical. The world stood still in those seconds. Its continuance seemed to hinge on the very sound that came out of their mouths. *"Going to the chapel and...married,"* they swayed as they sang. Soon she relaxed because the harmony was sweet and their steps came together like clockwork.

The crowd got into the groove and stood on their feet. They clapped along with them as they sang. No one could miss the Hobbstown following standing in the front row, shouting at the top of their lungs. It was clear as she watched the other Passionettes, consisting of her sister Diane, and sisters, Leslie and Cheryl Murdock, that this would be a night to remember. As they effortlessly performed their songs, she remembered the group's beginning.

It was the summer of 1964, and just for fun the four girls harmonized popular tunes at the Hobbstown park, at the bus stop, or sometimes at each other's home. Some of their favorites groups were the Shirelles, Marvelettes, Martha and the Vandellas, and the Supremes. Cheryl and Les were fourteen and thirteen years old. Cindy and Diane were sixteen and thirteen, respectively.

"You know, I believe you girls really got something," Nelson said one evening as they sang on the blacktop at the park. "A friend of mine, Fred Farmer, might be interested in hearing ya'll sing. He's a local record promoter from Springfield; got a recording studio right in his house. But I wouldn't want you all to go in for a demo with him until you really have more practice.

"The next step would be getting to Eddie Power, the talent promoter out of Newark who produces big shows at the Terrace Ballroom. I pretty much have that association through George Davidson too since he works with Eddie. But the first thing you all need is a manager. I believe I have the connections to get ya'll on the right circuit. The goal would be to open at the Terrace Ballroom for headliners like the Temptations, Supremes, any of the big names. That's how you get the exposure."

Cindy pinched herself more than a few times when Daddy and Mama allowed her and Diane to crisscross New Jersey along with the Murdock girls. They performed at various events, which on occasion included nightclubs. However, the

Richard Nelson

approval had not come without a host of rules to which Nelson, as everyone called Richard, readily agreed.

"I'm entrusting my daughters to your care at these singing shows," Daddy said to Nelson at the outset.

"Yes, sir, Mr. Nearo. Mr. Book said he'll be at most of the events; but if you want one of your boys to come along, too, that's fine."

"Didn't I tell you they a great group," the announcer said. The thunderous applause brought Cindy back to the show. "Give the Passionettes another hand, ladies and gentlemen. Them Supremes better watch out."

School was moving along at lightning pace. Cindy was voted into class council. Suddenly some of the students seemed to think it was hip to have a black friend. Still, she was wary of this new-found popularity since, except for a few, these were the same students to whom she had been invisible during grade school.

"Ya'll singing next door?" Cindy heard the elderly man ask Les as she walked ahead of them to the counter. They were performing at the Crossing Inn in Trenton, New Jersey. Nelson had stopped at the Kentucky Fried Chicken restaurant to buy some food before the show that Saturday evening. Cindy turned around to make sure Nelson was close by and saw that he was right behind Cheryl.

"Ya'll sure look pretty," the man continued to speak.

She noticed that everyone in the eatery kind of paused to check them out. A soft thrill went up her spine, as it did whenever they were acknowledged as performers, but somehow tonight seemed special. She didn't know if it was because they were hard to miss in their matching pink and blue paisley jumpsuits, or if they actually came across as a bonafide "girl group." But the night felt electric.

"Girls, what ya'll want to eat?" Cindy barely heard Nelson as she took in the flutter of interest in them at the restaurant.

"Oh, just a piece of chicken for me," she said.

"Me too," Diane said.

"Alright. I may as well get a twelve-piece," Nelson commented. "Cheryl, you want chicken?"

Cindy could see that Cheryl was enamored with the attention from the crowd. She wasn't sure if she heard Nelson. She nudged her with her elbow.

"Oh, yes, sir," Cheryl laughed, and then whispered to Cindy, "I'm so excited I can hardly breathe.

"So am I."

They sat down at a nearby empty table.

"Girls, just go out there and do your best, and you'll be fine," Nelson encouraged them. He passed them soda. "Like I been telling ya'll, the Crossing Inn crowd is a tough bunch. But it's one thing for sure, if they like the act that means we really have something as a group."

"Let's hurry up and eat so we can warm up with the band," Cheryl said. The Crossing Inn had an in-house band. Cindy could tell Cheryl was excited because her eyes danced. She had proved to be excellent as the group's choreographer.

"Well, we definitely want everything to be on the money," Nelson continued, "especially tonight. But you girls have been practicing hard every day, and I know you'll do great."

The thought of doing a bad show registered. All of a sudden Cindy couldn't wait to get in a few more rehearsals. She took a few bites of chicken so as not to waste Nelson's money. He always picked up the tab for dinner on show nights.

She looked up to see a teenage boy standing at their table. He smiled and thrust a pencil and paper at her.

"Can I have your autograph?" he asked shyly.

Her stomach did a blissful little cartwheel. This was the first time anyone had asked for an autograph, but she wasn't going to let anyone know that. "Sure," she said confidently, and after learning his name, she autographed the paper. She then passed the paper to Diane, as if she too had been signing autographs for years. She smiled and kicked her sister under the table so she wouldn't act overly surprised… like this had never happened before.

Diane gave her a look and laughed. "Oh yes, I'll be happy to autograph it," she said sweetly. Cindy almost burst out laughing.

"Me, too," Cheryl chimed in.

Les got in on the act. "Oh certainly," she said.

Cindy noticed how pretty Les looked; her skin was the color of honey. While they were all attractive girls, Les had a certain charisma. And she seemed to be the one who drew the most attention from the opposite sex as they traveled around the state.

She couldn't help but smile as she remembered probably the first time she visited the Murdock home, and Leslie introduced her to a "sugar sandwich." Cindy watched as Les mixed sugar and a little water in a cup until it was pasty. She then smoothed it over a slice of white bread and topped it with another piece of bread. "You want one, Cindy? Here you'll like it," she said as she cut the sandwich in half and handed half to Cindy. As she bit into the sandwich, Cindy thought the taste did not differ much from the syrup sandwiches that she and some of her siblings sometimes snacked on.

Now, as they concentrated on signing autographs she took them all in. Diane was a dead ringer for Mama's elegant beauty except that she wasn't tall. Cheryl was petite, with a velvety-smooth caramel complexion. As for Cindy's appearance, it had finally come together during her freshman year. Although she did not believe herself to be a natural beauty, she worked hard at looking her best. She scrubbed her face with water and a little rubbing alcohol every night. It gave her the clean look she desired when she put on makeup. Her hair was permed to perfection and she made sure her long fingernails were always impeccably polished.

After getting the job at Holland-Rantos, she regularly shopped at the Robert Hall clothing store across Route 22, and at Two Guys from Harrison in Watchung. Coupled with the clothing passed down from her older sisters, she dressed her lean, five-foot-seven frame in competition with the trendsetters at school. However, being a member of the Passionettes was the thing that made her spirit come alive. While it seemed that college was out of reach, she did believe the four of them were on their way to fame and fortune through song.

"Hey, we better get going," Les said. She stood up.

"Yeah, let's go," Nelson said.

Cindy was glad to hear him sound so jovial. It helped to ease her before-show jitters.

"I'll just take the food and save it for ya'll until after the performance," he added.

"Ya'll singing next door at the Crossing Inn?" one of the men behind the counter asked as they were almost at the door.

"Yes, sir," Nelson answered. "These are my girls, the Passionettes."

"Ladies and gentlemen, we have a sensational singing group for your entertainment tonight," the announcer shouted into the microphone. The group stood waiting in the wings backstage.

"Okay, let's get ready," Diane said. They held hands and said a quick prayer as the master of ceremony called their name.

After their last song, they joined Nelson at the table. He beamed, as cameras flashed. "You girls were great," he yelled over the noise. Many of the people in the audience came over to congratulate them on their performance. They signed more autographs. They were in with the Crossing Inn crowd.

"Okay, let's go over the steps one more time," Cheryl said. They practiced at the Murdock home that Friday evening.

Cindy saw Les frown. "I thought we were done," she said. "We've gone over this so many times, Cheryl. We know it like the back of our hands. Gee whiz."

"Les, we have to practice," Cheryl continued. "What about our show last Saturday at the Dreamboat? It was bad because we slacked off rehearsing."

The girls were about half an hour into practice. They usually went at least two hours, three times a week. Nelson's job as a mason made it hard for him to make all of the rehearsals. But they usually did a good job rehearsing on their own.

Somehow Cindy became the voice of reason in the group. She wasn't unhappy about it, but rather took it in stride since she was the eldest. Anyway, tonight she knew why everyone was anxious for practice to end. There was a cookout going on at the Hobbstown park that would last through the weekend. They were all eager for fun at the park before it got too late. It was tempting to rush through the rehearsal, but she agreed with Cheryl.

"Les, we'll never be great unless we put everything into our practice time," Cindy tried to sound persuasive. "We have to stay committed to make it big." But even as she heard herself giving words of encouragement her heart and mind were already at the park.

Diane sprang to her feet. "Okay, let's go ahead and finish our practice because we sure need it. I don't ever want to be embarrassed like we were at the Dreamboat last week."

Les shrugged her shoulders and smiled weakly. "Alright. Let's finish practice."

"I'm quitting the group," Les announced at the next rehearsal session. They were at the Williams' home.

What is she saying? Cindy couldn't believe her ears. The previously chatty room became curiously silent at this sudden news out of the blue. *She has to be joking.* But as she studied Les' face, she saw traces of melancholy.

"Somebody is always doing something wrong, hitting the wrong note or not being at practice on time. So I think it's best that I leave the group because I'm not perfect."

"Oh, Les, no. Nobody blames you for anything. We all mess up sometimes. I didn't realize it bothered you that much," Cindy said. "Girl, we can work it out, you know?"

However, inwardly she admitted there was tension in the group of late, but they had always gotten beyond it. She and Diane sang low and high soprano, while Cheryl and Les sang tenor and alto, respectively. There were moments when someone might be off-key, and after long hours of practice tempers sometimes flared over silly things. However, they had a great sound, and most of the time they ended up laughing and consoling each other when things got rough.

Diane sighed. "Les, we need you. Why don't you think about it? We have a good sound and every group has internal problems sometimes. But like Cindy said, we can work them out."

Cheryl stood quietly.

"I'm sorry ya'll," Les sounded sad but determined, "but I just can't continue. I know you'll find someone to take my place. Honestly, I've been thinking about leaving for a while. I'm sorry." She quietly walked out the door.

They sat for the longest time, stunned. *What would we do now without Les?* Cindy thought. *It would seem strange to have a three-person group. But I can't imagine anyone taking Les' place. Maybe she'll change her mind and come back.*

The group had prepared relentlessly for the talent show taking place at Somerville High that night. They were confident they would blast the roof off the house and take first prize. Much to their disappointment, Leslie did not return to the group. Joyce Hobbs, who sang contralto, joined the Passionettes. In addition, Larry Brown, a former member of the Parliament, started giving the Passionettes impromptu voice lessons. He hailed from Plainfield, New Jersey, and became the sometimes-fifth member of the group.

Backstage was packed with local talent. There was an excitement in the air that they had never experienced. It felt as if they were on the verge of something big; like fame was just within their grasp.

"Hey, listen," Nelson said, appearing more anxious than Cindy could ever remember, "there are talent scouts in the audience tonight. I made sure somebody from Eddie Power Productions would be here. This is a big opportunity. All you have to do is sing your best, and we might get a contract."

Although they now had a more polished sound because of Larry's professional savvy, it had cost them. They had lost that "all-girl" sugary sound that they were becoming known for. *Yet, she told herself, Larry is a seasoned performer and we should be honored that he took up with us after his split from the Parliament. After all, they had a number one hit, "I Wanna Testify."* She remembered how Larry was taken with them as they sang in the Hobbstown park after a baseball game one evening.

"You girls can sing," he said. "You got something special."

She smiled now remembering how thrilled they were when he showed interest in them. She knew there was a lot of local competition that he could have gone with, especially Van Turner's group, the Dream Hearts of Somerville. The group featured Tina Downs, and she could "sang." There was also the Teachers Plus Three of New Brunswick, and Connie Hobbs was a lead singer with that group. The Admirations of Plainfield were also a force to be reckoned with. But she comforted herself with the fact that Larry said he saw something unique in them.

"Oh my God, they sound so good," Cheryl exclaimed as the

Dream Hearts sang "Smoke Gets in Your Eyes." The song floated through the air with such power and clarity that it took Cindy's breath away.

"Um...they sound great," Cindy agreed. And for the first time that night she felt edgy.

"Yeah, they sound good, but we sound better," Larry said. "We'll blow them away."

I hope you're right, Cindy thought, but said nothing.

"Passionettes, get ready. You're up next," somebody shouted.

Cindy smoothed her hair and skirt. Tonight they were not dressed in matching outfits. Since it was an after-school event, everyone dressed in the same clothing they wore to school that day. The microphone was powerful. From the first note their harmony bounced flawlessly from one huge wall of the auditorium to the next. *We never sounded better.* Cindy felt more confident after they finished the first verse. *No band, just our voices blending together like fine gold.*

———

"Get off the stage," the police officer said as he came toward the Passionettes from backstage. At the same time, Cindy realized that there were other policemen in the aisles of the auditorium. "Everyone out," they shouted. "Show's over." The group reluctantly left the stage.

"What's going on, officer?" Larry asked.

"Please just disperse from the auditorium," the officer shouted.

They were devastated. Behind the scenes they learned a fight broke out in the auditorium and that was the reason the remainder of the show was canceled. They had floated on that stellar cloud of what was sure to have been their best performance to date. But it had swiftly come to an end. They were all full of tears, but most of all it was obvious that no contract would come to them that night.

It was December 4, 1965. When the telephone rang that morning, its sense of urgency was undeniable. It woke Cindy from a restless sleep.

"Oh, no," she heard Mama's voice rise in disbelief to whomever was on the phone. A shiver went through her body. "I'm so sorry, Nonie," Mama continued. "I'll be over as quick as I can."

Lizzie, she thought, as she trembled under the bedcovers that had been warm just a few moments ago. *This can't be happening. Nobody dies at nineteen.* Lizzie was hospitalized with pneumonia. She remembered the oxygen tent that barely allowed her to breathe, and she squeezed back the rush of tears that came to her eyes. But now it was apparent that it did not save her. She jumped out of bed, hoping that what she thought she heard was not true. She saw the troubled look on Mama's face.

"Mama, what happened?" she asked shakily. However, before she could answer, the previously sleepy home was overcome with children crying in disbelief. It was unbelievable; *beautiful Lizzie with the long thick tresses was gone.*

As she peeked through the living room drapes the cars already lined up at the Tukes' home was a heartbreaking sign that death had come to their dwelling. It looked cold and gloomy outside, a reflection of her heart, and she sorrowfully let the curtain go. She felt the sun had surely turned its back on them; there was no warmth anywhere. It stayed in for a season, and the stars that she and her friends knew so well they had given them names, now seemed distant and unapproachable. The circle of youth was broken forever.

It was April 1967.

"Joyce, please complete the homework problem from last night." Mr. G's voice cut through the air like a sharp-edged knife. Cindy looked up from her seat in the back row of the class.

Joyce flipped through the book. She gave the teacher an answer.

"That is not the correct problem, Miss Hobbs," he said.

Cindy listened with growing concern. *He is really angry*, she thought.

"Complete the correct homework problem," he demanded. And then he yelled at Joyce. "Can't you speak? Do you have your homework assignment or not?"

Joyce was in tears, and she jumped up and ran from the room. Mr. G followed her. "You will come back to class now, young lady, or receive detention," he yelled as he followed her. The class became as silent as a morgue and everything could be heard from the hallway.

"Come out of that bathroom," Mr. G bellowed. Cindy flinched as he banged loudly on the door.

What is going on? she wondered. *Why is he so upset?*

"Young lady, get out here right now," he ranted, "or receive detention."

Joyce had shared with Cindy that since graduation would take place in just a few months she took on more hours at her after-school job at the Grand Union grocery store. So Cindy thought she probably just did not have the time to complete the homework assignment.

Suddenly, Mr. G came back to the classroom. He panted as if he were out of breath. His face flushed shades of scarlet. He sat down and began writing.

"Class, continue studying the homework assignment from last night. I'll return in a few minutes," he said. With that, he ripped out the sheet of paper and walked out of the door.

Joyce did not return to school.

Cindy later asked Joyce why she didn't come back to school when they were so close to graduation.

"It became impossible because I got a few days detention from that incident," Joyce explained. "The detention made me late for work. So when I went to work instead of detention the second day, weeks were added on to the detention, and after a while, I just couldn't keep up with both."

———

Graduation day was almost upon them. Classes for seniors were over by 2:00 p.m.

"Cindy Lou, will you sign my yearbook?" Jug asked. They were in study hall. Time had softened her hurt feelings toward Jug. She knew it also had something to do with the fact that soon she would step out from under the school environment's never-ending microscope.

"Only if you'll sign mine," she answered.

As they laughed, she admitted it felt good to laugh with him again. They exchanged books. When he handed her yearbook back to her he suddenly looked serious.

"Honestly, I wish we could start over from eighth grade. I would do things differently," he said.

After all these years is he really going to apologize? she wondered.

Jug continued. "We had fun together. You were a good friend, and I ruined it. I wish there was some way to change that, and I'm sorry."

They stared at each other for the longest time. She wondered what she should say now. This was the apology that would have meant so much so many years ago. She had once felt their friendship was color blind, and understood that was why the incident had seared her heart so completely.

"I wish you the best in everything, Jug. I was pretty stubborn too. Hey, we were just kids, and we all make mistakes. I'm sorry, too."

Her eyes misted when Jug leaned over and placed his arm around her shoulder. But ghostly remembrances of him in blackface still overshadowed this moment in time of forgiveness. It was too late. *The nine-to-five-like school-day friendships are over,* she thought, *and we'll probably never see each other again.*

"Take good care of yourself," he said. "Always be happy."

She also realized that her time with her close circle of friends, Etta, Kate, Bonnie and Doreen (they became friends again after the fight), was about to come to an end. During senior year, Doreen was like the Doreen of old. However, two months before graduation she showed Cindy the truism of the poet's words; "the more things change, the more they stay the same."

"Vinnie and I are getting married," Doreen said to Cindy during study hall. "You know I want to invite you to the wedding because you are a good friend. You know that, don't you, Cin?"

"Yes. Sure, Doreen. I know that." She felt that old irritation creep over her where Doreen was concerned and just wanted her to get to the point. "What's the matter?"

"Well, Vinnie's folks are Italian. They don't like black people, so you won't be able to come."

The hairs practically stood up on her head as anger coursed through her being. *Won't be able to come,* she wanted to scream at Doreen. *What makes you think I want to go to your wedding just because you're white?* But she bit her tongue, finding solace in the fact that the facade was nearly over.

"I understand, Doreen. When are you getting married?"

"Well, I've already quit school," Doreen laughed. "I just want to be barefoot and pregnant."

How ironic, Cindy thought. *She's white and she can easily go to college, yet she chose to quit school.*

"I'll see you around, Doreen."

They hugged quickly. Cindy couldn't get away fast enough.

"We'll keep in touch," Doreen said.

Kate and Etta fussed with their hair. They were getting ready to step into cap and gown on graduation day. Bonnie and Cindy were ready and stood nearby.

"I can't believe this day is here," Bonnie said.

Cindy felt weepy as the two wrote the equivalent of a paragraph in each other's yearbook. There was so much to say; she found herself fighting back tears. Although circumstances brought her in close contact with the clique, she understood in her heart of hearts that they had been surface friends. Bonnie was her true-blue and vice-versa.

"I'm really gonna miss you, Bon," she said.

Bonnie burst into tears. "I'm gonna miss you more. Remember second grade, when you didn't like me," she said. They both laughed.

"You'll smear your eye makeup if you keep crying," Cindy said. She swallowed deeply to hold back her own tears.

Ms. Fats came through the door and Cindy consoled herself that she would never again have to look at those tightly-drawn lips, as if the whole world was sour.

"Line up girls, it's time to march," she said. They formed a row and Ms. Fats began her traditional walk down the winding row of students. She congratulated and embraced each student. *Well,* Cindy thought as Ms. Fats came near, *I have stepped into Mary Nell's shoes. Just let her snub me. Just let her put her hand out. I swear I will keep my hands to my side.*

But to Cindy's amazement, when Ms. Fats got to her she hugged her warmly and whispered, "Congratulations, Cindy. You're a hard worker. You're going to do well in life."

Cindy and her brother Frank were the only black graduates in their 1967 class of approximately 400 students.

In late 1967 the Passionettes had grown pretty tight with the Admirations, which consisted of brothers Richard, Frankie, John Joseph (Jo Jo) Boyce, and Rochelle Eure. Larry Brown abruptly disappeared from the scene and everyone breathed a sigh of relief. He had pushed them relentlessly. And Cindy knew Nelson had become unhappy with Larry's overly aggressive singing sessions with the group.

However, they found that the Admirations were in their corner. They were as hungry as the Passionettes to soar, and the groups gravitated to one another in a common bond. The Admirations were hot...they were in big demand. Cindy prayed that some of their stardust might fall on their group. Frankie offered to play guitar behind the Passionettes if his group didn't have a gig at the same time, and they were ecstatic.

———

"Listen up, girls. We got a contract for this big show coming to Franklin High School. You girls will be opening for the Soul Survivors." Nelson appeared more excited than Cindy ever remembered seeing him.

"You mean the group with the hit 'Expressway to Your Heart'?" Cheryl screamed. "Oh, my goodness. I can't believe it."

"Yep," Nelson said with a smile from ear to ear. "That's the group. There will be other acts, including the Teachers, Plus Three. But the Passionettes will go on right before the Soul Survivors. The Boyce brothers already said they would play for us that night. Ya'll have to practice every night until the show," he said. "No excuses."

"What will we sing?" Diane asked.

Cindy could tell she was wound up like a spring because she jumped to her feet. Diane could never sit still when she was excited.

"When is the show?" Cindy asked. She was already trying to envision what they would wear that night. *We'll definitely need new outfits*, she thought.

"The show is October 30, two weeks away," Nelson said. "Each group is scheduled to sing two selections. I thought Joyce could lead 'Maybe' 'cause ya'll already put a lot of practice into that song. And you sing it so well."

Cindy saw Joyce's eyes grow big with anticipation, accompanied by her deep, almost silent chuckle. "Well, let's get started," she said. "I'm ready."

"What about 'Look in My Eyes' for the second selection?" Cheryl asked. "We always do a good job on that song. Plus, we have our dance routines down for those numbers."

They all agreed that those would be their two songs for that night.

"We heard you ladies are going to blow us off the stage tonight," one of the Soul Survivors yelled over the wall. It was the night of the big show at Franklin High. Cindy wrestled with the butterflies doing the "Bump" in her stomach. They were in the girl's locker room of the gym changing for the performance. The Soul Survivors dressed in the boy's locker room. The girls giggled uncontrollably but, butterflies and all, Cindy knew they should show they were up for the challenge.

"Well, you can bet they'll dig us when we sing, but they'll forget about us as soon as you all take the stage," she didn't want them to think the Passionettes were arrogant.

"Oh, you think so, huh?" was the faceless retort. "Well, guys, we better get some autographs now. Then we can at least say we performed with the Passionettes."

Cindy could feel the creepy-crawlers in her belly recede into nothingness as they kidded back and forth. *They seem easy enough to like,* she thought. But she began to fret that Frankie and Richie hadn't made it there yet. *Well, that's what we get for bragging,* she lamented.

"Where are they?" she asked Nelson.

"They'll be here," he said confidently. "Don't worry. Three acts have to go on before ya'll."

"Don't panic, sis," Diane said. "Frankie practiced with us all week. You know if they agreed to do it, they'll be here."

"Yeah, it's still early," Joyce added.

Cindy felt better when Cheryl nodded her head in affirmation with the others. Yet, thoughts of the never-to-be-forgotten talent show of a few years back crept into her mind and she froze. Although they sang *a cappella* many times, tonight it was vital that a band back them up. All the other groups had bands. *Besides*, she thought, *people like to dance to the beat of the music.*

"You girls look so beautiful you'll knock 'em dead with that alone," one of the Soul Survivors said. They were talking face-to-face now backstage. But Cindy knew better; looks might help, but the crowd paid to hear great singing. She was pleased with how neat they looked in their new matching dresses. They wore lilac-colored, sleeveless, chiffon dresses. The outfits sported one large silk bow in the bodice of the same color. Nelson sprang for the outfits as he sometimes did. He would recoup his money after receiving payment for the show.

"He's right, you know," Nelson cut into Cindy's thoughts. "You all never looked prettier."

As Cindy eyed Diane, she marveled at how much her sister resembled a beautiful Barbie doll. The two had flitted around half the day with their hair. Finally, they settled on beehives with straight bangs. Joyce's thick hair fell just beneath her ears in a smooth pageboy; Cheryl's hair was impeccably tapered short in the back with full bangs. They helped each other with makeup, and tonight Cindy believed they had done a flawless job. Suddenly the backstage doors swung open and in walked Frankie and Ritchie. They were loaded down with band equipment. The Teachers Plus Three had just taken the stage. *Thank you, God,* Cindy breathed a rocky sigh of relief.

———

"May a be, if I cried every night..." Joyce sang and Cindy squeezed her eyes shut with emotion; Joyce sounded like an angel. She took a deep breath and belted out the background lyrics along with Diane and Cheryl, *"Oh, oh, maybe...may be."* *Perfect harmony*, she thought. *We got it.* She smiled to herself. She felt giddy as the crowd went wild when they mixed their dance

The Passionettes
From left to right, Richard Boyce, Cindy Williams, Cheryl
Murdock, Diane Williams, Frankie Boyce, Joyce Hobbs

routine to the song. Frankie ran his fingers up and down the lead guitar, his bright smile told her that they had hit a home run. Richard jammed on the bass guitar, cool, calm and collected, and everything was under control.

The crowd screamed their names. "Sing it," they yelled. Some clamored for the stage.

So this is how it feels, Cindy thought. It was a natural high and she wanted to float on that blissful cloud forever. By the time they finished singing 'Look in My Eyes,' she was persuaded that there could be nothing sweeter than performing. They were called back to the stage three times and each time they bowed the auditorium erupted with thunderous applause. *This must be Heaven*, Cindy concluded. *This is the life for me.*

Backstage there were warm hugs and laughter. She could see the other girls overflowed with happiness, too. Nelson was beside himself with joy.

"Ya'll took that show away from everybody tonight!" he exclaimed. "Even with that hit the Soul Survivors sang, ya'll stole the show. This is the start of something mighty big," he said.

The look on the faces of the other girls told Cindy that they were equally convinced. *We are on our way to the Terrace Ballroom just as sure as the sun shines every day.*

When Frankie entered the room at the Murdock house not too many months after the Franklin High School show, Cindy laid her pen down. She stood up and followed his eyes with a question as he gave her a bear-hug so tight she gasped for air.

"Hey, we got the contract with Warner Brothers Records," he shouted. "Hitsville Factory." Instant chaos broke out in the room as the girls joined in with screams of excitement. There were hugs all around.

"Wow, that was fast," Cheryl laughed as Frankie hugged her. "You all just cut the demo for them a few days ago didn't you?"

The Admirations
From top to bottom: Richard Boyce, Frankie Boyce,
Jo-Jo Boyce, Rochelle Eure

Frankie laughed. "Yeah, but those few days felt like forever."

They were thrilled. Cindy thought of how this would change the Admirations' lives. Perhaps their group would not be far behind. They were practicing songs she had written for an upcoming recording session in Springfield before Frankie came in. She was overjoyed that Nelson thought the songs were good enough to use if a contract came out of the demo.

"Where are the rest of the guys?" Joyce asked Frankie.

"I'm getting ready to catch up with those cats in a few minutes. We got a gig tomorrow evening so we'll be practicing late into the night."

"Oh boy, this is such good news," Diane cried. "You guys are going to make it big, Frankie. I can feel it."

"Di', I'm startin' to believe that myself," he said. "Hey, but we're gonna help ya'll too, you got that? That's a promise. Cindy, go ahead and put the finishing touches on the songs and we'll rehearse them next week."

"Oh, Frankie, you won't have time to do all that for us. You'll be too busy recording," Cindy said.

"If I'm lying, I'm flying," Frankie laughed. "Get it together for next week, okay? I'll be here. All we have to worry about is the arrangements for our album. Warner Brothers is gonna use some of the songs I wrote for the album. But the album won't come out until '68. Okay. Check ya'll later. Be cool," and he was gone into the night.

When Dr. Martin Luther King was assassinated on April 4, 1968, it was a time of great turbulence for Hobbstown's youth, as it was all over the nation. This came on the heels of the killing of Malcolm X in 1965, which had also been a time of shock and sorrow.

There was a deep sense of dread when the National Guard came to Somerville in riot gear since there were numerous outbreaks of rioting in Plainfield and Newark. However, there was no rioting in Somerville. All the while, the Vietnam War was raging in the background. When Lit enlisted in the Armed Services, everything seemed to be changing so quickly. Simultaneously, Richard and Frankie were both drafted into the Army before the Admirations album-in-progress was completed. As a result, all of the production plans were put on hold.

Frankie was his usual jovial self when he bid them so long. But his eyes were not persuasive. "We'll be back here before you know it, ready to finish the album," he reassured his friends just before being shipped off to a foreign land. "Yep, we'll pick up right where we left off."

It was December 21, 1968.

Bam. Bam. Bam!

Cindy heard someone knock on their back door that morning as though they would break it down. When she opened the door, Little Henry walked into the house as if he was in a trance.

"What's the matter, Little Henry?" she pushed the terror that suddenly engulfed her back, as she took in his countenance, especially his eyes. They looked ghostly.

"What's wrong, man?" Nearo, Jr. asked as he ran into the kitchen.

But Little Henry did not speak. Instead, tears rolled down his face and he shook his head from side to side. Cindy felt suddenly cold and pulled her robe tight. By this time everyone in the house had come to the kitchen to see what was going on. The telephone rang. Nearo picked it up.

"What?" he exclaimed into the phone. "Leslie? Oh no…what happened? Got hit by a car? Oh, my God."

Cindy wanted to run away, but the need for truth rooted her to the spot. Her brother looked shocked, and Little Henry was in a state of melancholy that she had not witnessed before. *This can not be happening,* she prayed. Suddenly her feet came unglued and she bolted to her room. *If I can just get to the Murdock house,*

I'll see that everything is alright. Maybe Les was hurt badly, but not dead, she reasoned.

She and Diane ran the shortcut through the Bell's backyard to Sussex Avenue. Cindy saw the ominous host of cars that lined the street next to the Murdock home. They continued their trek towards the house. Weeping and moaning met them on the little trail they had run so many times to and from the home. Her heart sank. She looked at her sister and as their eyes met her heart gave way to that icy empty feeling that comes with knowing death.

Ms. Anna sat at her kitchen table. "I begged her not to walk North Bridge Street last night," she said. "But she kept saying she wanted to get some fresh air. It was so cold and dark last night. A car came along and hit her, and with all those ditches by the time they found her she had drowned."

"Ms. Anna, I saw Les walking last night on my way into town," Cindy was incredulous. "I offered her a ride, but she said she wanted to walk."

"Oh, my Leli," Ms. Anna said softly. "Several people said they saw her and offered her a ride. I just wish she had taken a ride with someone."

They sat quietly as the house filled with childhood friends and neighbors. Cheryl was encumbered with tears. "First my father, now my sister," she said softly to them.

Cindy felt both grieved and troubled. *I should have been more persuasive,* she thought sadly. But she also knew that no amount of hindsight would bring lovely Leslie back.

Ms. Fats' recommendation to take typing had not been in vain. In 1968 Cindy landed a secretarial job at Research-Cottrell in Peapack. She breezed through the typing test and vowed this would be her escape from factory work. It was ironic, since a few years earlier she was on cloud nine as she believed her career would be performing. But lately she could not shake the feeling that the Passionettes were spiraling downward.

"It's just really hard right now," Cheryl said one night as they practiced. "I can't even think straight sometimes, let alone sing."

During these times no one said much. Cindy knew it was because they were all despondent. It was as if she could feel the group dying. The demo session had gone badly. They had slacked off practicing because of their social lives. The group was on-again, off-again. And she knew that, although he didn't say it, Nelson had to be tired of dealing with all of their issues. But she couldn't say that to Cheryl. *I have to fulfill my role as the voice of reason*, she reminded herself.

"You'll see, Cheryl," she said as cheerfully as she could muster. "When Frankie comes home from 'Nam things will change. Just hang in there." But even as she said the words, in her heart she did not feel it. The Terrace Ballroom dream had faded into oblivion.

The winter of 1969 arrived with frigid winds that chilled to the bone. Cindy ran the trail from the Bryant house to her home with a scarf securely wrapped around her neck and face.

"It's freezing out there," she said to no one in particular when she entered the house. As she removed her scarf she saw Diane standing in the kitchen. She was pale; her eyes were red, as though she had been crying. A familiar icy feeling came over Cindy. *Where was everyone this Sunday?* she wondered. Although most of her older brothers and sisters now lived on their own, the house was usually full of noise with their Sunday visits. However, today the house was eerily quiet.

"Cint, you better sit down," Diane said.

But she couldn't sit down. That would mean she was giving Diane permission to tell her some bad news that she did not want to hear. She backed up towards the front door. *If I go out and come back, I'll see that this isn't happening. I'm dreaming.* Suddenly, every superstition that she had ever heard in the town as a child rushed in: "You know death comes in threes," "Step on a crack, break your mother's back," and so on and so on.

Diane came towards her.

"Don't tell me, Diane." A vision of Lit in Vietnam raced through her mind. She tried to push the thought away.

Tears streamed down Diane's face and she embraced her sister. "Frankie's dead. He was killed in battle."

The world stopped. "No, not Frankie, Diane, not Frankie," she cried, but deep within she knew it was true. *All of those beautiful songs he wrote would never be heard. What will we do without Frankie? There could never be anyone as wonderful and kind as Frankie.*

It was January 20, 1969, the same day Richard Millhouse Nixon was ushered in as President of the United States.

———

Chapter 8

The Martin Luther King Youth Center and the Somerville Raiders

Hobbstown had seen some rough times. The underlying need for acceptance could not be fulfilled by one evening a week at the local Fisherman Teen club. The younger children sought a community outlet within Hobbstown minus the weekday racial divide at school. At the same time, the Somerville Raiders' baseball team was in full swing.

"We can raise money to build our own recreational center. Perhaps name it after Martin Luther King," Chester, Jr. suggested. The young folk had just wrapped up a huge bonfire at the park. They lingered at the blacktop and talked. It was the summer of 1969.

"There has never been a social outlet for the kids of Hobbstown," Chet continued.

"Well, they do have the Fisherman club on Friday nights," someone chimed in.

Cindy wasn't gung-ho about the Fisherman club. It was a Friday night teen club located in a local church in Somerville. While it was a place they could let their hair down, it was as racially divided as a school day. For the most part, the black teens stayed in one section and the whites remained in another. She spoke up.

"No. The Fisherman is like every other social setting in the area. The majority is always white. Sure, we can go if we want to, but we all know we aren't genuinely welcome. That's how it's always been. It would be wonderful for the kids coming up now to have a hangout right here in Hobbstown."

"Look at all the barbecues and fund-raisers the Raiders give, bus rides to Coney Island and hay-rides," Chet explained. "That's how our team raises money for uniforms and any general needs of the players. We can do the same to build a youth center out here."

DJ spoke up. He was home from the armed services. "It will take a whole lot more than what might be raised from cookouts. We're talking major capital. If we start a project it will have to be a serious effort to have any merit."

"Why don't we put on a play to raise some money?" Diane asked. "We're all familiar with the play *Buzz Riley's Back in Town*. There are enough of us kids out here to do it. Maybe we can even put the play on at the high school."

Cindy smiled as she remembered how the young teens put on tidbits of this musical comedy off and on around the neighborhood over the years.

"Yeah, that's a good idea, Diane." Little Henry sounded enthused.

"We definitely need our own thing," Harry agreed.

Diane's face glowed with enthusiasm when she came from school that evening.

"They want us to take the play to Bucks County, Pennsylvania," Diane said to the family. The kids had already put the play on at Bridgewater-West High. It had been a huge success. Diane and Little Henry were the main characters of *Buzz Riley's Back in Town*. They were both vocally powerful.

However, many of the young teens of Hobbstown also participated in the play.

Chet was at the house as well. He spent so much time with Cindy's brothers that he was more like a brother than a cousin. Cathy, his sister, was close in age to Lanie.

Diane was about to burst from excitement. "Somebody white from Bucks County was at the play. They liked it so much they wanted to know if we would be interested in putting the play on there."

"Hot dog," Chet said. "That should bring in some serious money."

After the smashing financial success of the Bucks County production of *Buzz Riley's Back in Town*, the push was on for the dream. It gave the Hobbstown teens real hope. They went right to work on what was billed as a "Soul Show" to bring in more funds for the MLK Youth Center project.

"Let's get a band together for the soul show," Ernie Van Ness suggested one day as the teens bantered ideas back and forth. They practiced at the park and at various homes in Hobbstown. The band included Ernie Van Ness, Tyrone Stackhouse and a few other guys from Hobbstown. Finally the show opened to the public on a warm summer weekend, accompanied by the sale of "soul food" to compliment the show.

Tom sang his trademark song, "Soul Train, Night Train." There were other performances, but Little Henry's rendition of "Fingertips" was the pinnacle of the night. As she watched him, Cindy reflected on how he had slowly but surely returned to his fun loving self after Leslie's death. He danced now in a passionate heat. His moves were a combination of James Brown and Jackie Wilson, and he kept the crowd on their feet. The show brought in $600 towards the MLKY Center project.

"We're canvassing the neighborhood to raise more money for building the center," Ian said to Cindy. She and some of the Stackhouse girls stood at the Williams' front door. The Stackhouse family had long lived in Hobbstown. The Van Ness family now lived up the street on Monmouth Avenue, and the Jewett's were on Stewart's Hill. The Jewett's were related to the Stackhouse family.

"Really, right now?" she asked.

"Yep. We split up from the guys," Bunny said. "Wade, Charles, Kenny, Kevin, and some of the other boys are canvassing down the street and on Sussex Avenue. We decided to start soliciting up the street and then head to Woodlawn Avenue. There's about four or five carloads. We're going all over Bridgewater Township looking for donations."

"The bake sale at Macedonia is next week. And all the proceeds will go into the pot for the project, too," Ian added.

‘That's my boy," Ms. Gertrude shouted from her seat in the bleachers. Howard Robinson rounded the bases like a gazelle and slid his long lean body into home plate.

"Safe!" the umpire bellowed. The fans of the Somerville Raiders' ball club went wild with glee. It had been a close game, but the Raiders pulled off a magnificent win and garnered their first championship. It was 1970.

The advent of the Raiders' team had a positive effect on Hobbstown, for they sorely needed something upbeat to hold on to. Cindy watched Ms. Gertrude as she merrily embraced her son.

"Me and your Aunt Claretha got food in the trunk of the car," she laughed. "It's still nice and warm. Tell the other boys to come on over and help themselves."

Before he could respond, however, fellow teammates heaved

"Big Rob" into the air. He was a six-foot-five, 190-pound, dark-skinned handsome guy in his mid-twenties.

"Hey, let's sing the tribute song," Naomi Miller shouted.

It took a whole lot of doing, but they did it.
Yes, they did ya'll.
It took Robby on the mound, and Andy cuttin' 'em down.
Yes, they did it.
Yes, they did ya'll.
It took Pitt to get a hit, and then Nova
to throw a fit, but they made it.
Yes, they did ya'll.

As the crowd laughed and sang, Cindy thought of how good it felt to sing along with the crowd with no expectations for perfection. The song, written by Naomi and her sisters Anna, Hannah, Molly, and niece, Linda Murdock had quickly become the Raiders' anthem.

Richard Nelson walked up. He was manager of the team, and he burst with pride over winning the championship. "Hey, let's get this celebration started," he said. "The other team is hosting the after-party at the lounge. Let's go."

Ms. Gertrude laughed. "Well, just like we don't miss no games, we don't miss no after-parties neither," she said. "We'll drive on over there. They can add this food to what they already got."

The members of the all-black Somerville Raiders' team hailed mostly from Somerville and Hobbstown. Their games became one of the big attractions of the summer when they joined the semi-pro Montclair Garden State Baseball League. Hobbstown and Somerville religiously followed the hometown boys as if they were in the major league. The members included Richard Nelson, Nearo Williams, Jr., Joe, James and Otis Harris, Chet

Williams, Jr., Jesse Evans, Almas Smith, Robert and Wade Bryant, Leroy Jones, Sylvester Pitt, Gary, Roy, Russell and Andy Murdock, III, Grover Lewis, Howard Robinson, Tim Brooks, Jerry Stackhouse, Philip and David Miller, Charles Ryles, Arscko Raines, George Gainey, Robert Davis, Joel Hobbs, Charlie and David Jones, and Al Davidson.

When the Raiders hosted after-parties they pulled out all the stops. Preparations began on Friday and culminated on Sunday with the game. As usual, the Hobbstown park teemed with children and adults.

"Let's get two grills going," Nelson said. Cindy smiled because it was nice to see the blissful look of anticipation on his face. It reminded her of the earlier days when they were singing. "We got 100 pounds of chicken and ribs to grill and sell," he laughed.

"We need to round up some more bins for the drinks," someone said. "Man, a lot of people donated so much stuff."

Nelson wiped beads of perspiration on his forehead with a cloth and jammed it in his pocket. "Well, like they say, can't nobody host a game or after-party like the Raiders. Even the weather is cooperating…not a cloud in the sky."

———

It was a double header that weekend. Hobbstown's park was packed with hometown supporters and followers of the competing team. Nearo was the relief pitcher.

"Look at him, Nearo," Phil shouted as Nearo wound up the pitch. "You can tell he can't hit just by looking at him." This put the hometown in stitches. Clearly Phil was the emotional heartbeat of the team.

Nearo looked to first base—the fake—then he glided the ball home.

"Strike," the umpire shouted. "He's oouut!"

———

It was the bottom of the seventh inning. Chet was at bat. The bases were loaded with two outs. Phil was on third base. "Make it sing, Chet," Phil yelled towards home plate. "You know you can make that ball hum right out of this park like a song."

"Ball two," the umpire shouted.

The crowd was suddenly silent. The throw left the pitcher's hand.

Crack, as bat met ball.

"It's outta here," Cindy heard someone yell. She watched as the ball soared like an eagle, lofty and unreachable. The outfield fruitlessly backed up. Chet scrambled all the way to third, while all the runners on base came home.

"Come on home, Chet," the crowd yelled. Phil jumped up and down near home plate. "You got it, Chet," he screamed.

Chet ran from third and slid into home like a shot from a cannon. Simultaneously, the powerful throw came to home plate.

"Safe!" the umpire shouted.

————

The MLK Youth Center project needed leadership. Helen Tukes was nominated president of the Somerville Manor Civic Association. This non-profit organization originated during the heavy campaigns by the youth for donations toward building a youth center. Meetings were held at Macedonia Baptist Church.

"Let's come to order," Helen announced at the meeting that evening. "We have a lot to discuss tonight. So far, the Civic Association has received a little over $4,000 through pledges from residents of Bridgewater Township towards the MLK Youth Center project. Hobbstown's door-to-door effort raised $2,000. Ms. Favor is going to fill us in now about area church pledges and various company contributions. You have all done a fantastic job with the fund-raising effort."

"Good evening, everyone," Ms. Favor began. Margaret

Favor was white and, as fate would have it, had just retired from her job with the Bridgewater Township Borough. As she spoke, Cindy was struck by her sincerity; she was a key person in driving the youth center project forward.

"I am so happy to give this report," Ms. Favor continued. "We have over seventeen sponsoring churches and temples that have pledged $15,000 towards the building effort."

A huge round of applause followed. Ms. Favor laid out the financial status. Many progressive area whites put their blood, sweat, and tears into the project alongside the folks from Hobbstown. In addition to Margaret Favor, Shuny Goldrich, Carol and Michael Goodsen, and R. Thiele were heavy supporters. They participated on the Board of Directors and were well-known in the township.

Cindy looked around the room at the attendees. *It's possible that our younger siblings might soon have the opportunity to enjoy a social arena that eluded us as youngsters,* she thought. Robert, Wade, and Charles Bryant, Diane, Frank and Lena, Sheila, Karen, and Janice Williams, Chet Williams, Ian Gould, Lutherene Miller, the Hobbs boys, some of the Stackhouse kids, Tom and Betty Tukes, the Bell boys, Cheryl, Gary, and Russell Murdock, Ernie, Edna, and Marcy Van Ness, Ken Hobbs, and Kevin Proctor. They were all active members of the Civic Association, among others. As they listened, the air was charged with extraordinary energy.

"I also have a handout of area businesses that have pledged to make substantial contributions to the building effort. Just to name a few: Charles Hobbs & Sons; Richard Nelson, general contractor; Raritan Valley Engineering; and Branchburg Truss & Component Co. It's a fairly extensive list so please read it in the document at your leisure."

"Ms. Favor, thank you very much for your report." Helen had the floor again. "We should find out in a few months the status of the proposal to the Bridgewater Borough for land to build the construction. As we've shared many times, the square footage we're requesting is 1,500 square feet. Our proposal also requests that the building be located in Hobbstown. It's been a long road, and we still have some hurdles to climb."

"Yes," Ms. Goodsen spoke up, "but look how far we've come. I have no doubt we will get there."

"Here, here," came affirmative responses from the group.

"Helen, before we close, can we read the mission statement?" Wade asked. "I think it's important for us to read our mission statement at every meeting so we don't lose sight of why the building is so important."

"Sure," Helen responded. "That's a good idea. After all the time we spent putting the mission statement together, we better make sure we know it." Everyone laughed. "Let's all read it together."

"'The center's mission seeks to fulfill the dream of the man for which it is named by providing a positive learning atmosphere for our future leaders. To make a difference in the lives of both our students and their families through our mission of providing high-quality child-care services in a safe and healthy environment for children from all ethnic backgrounds in need of our services.'"

It was September 1971 and the Raiders were hosting their annual end-of-season barbecue at the Hobbstown Park. When Cindy got out of her car to drop off some refreshments she could tell the usual grits-and-gravy atmosphere prevailed. It was mid-morning, but already scorching enough to fry an egg on the pavement.

"Here's the potato salad," she said to Nelson, and placed the large container on a nearby table.

"Great. Thank the family for us," Nelson said happily. "We'll put it on ice."

John Proctor, Sr. helped Nelson get the grills fired up. He lifted the top from the huge pot on the grill. "Ump, them must be

Nonie's collard greens," he said. "She know she can fix some good collards." He placed the top back on the huge pot with a laugh.

"Yeah, can't nobody cook greens like Ms. Nonie," Nelson agreed.

"Big Rob threw that ball nearly 100 miles an hour," one of the players bragged as they set up.

"Yeah, Rob probably could have made the majors if it could have been pursued. He's a mighty fine pitcher," Nelson commented. "And Andy sure is a good catcher. Don't many balls get by him. He gets better and better each year. And whenever Gary and Nearo relief-pitch, they always right on the money."

Rob walked up. "Well," he said slowly, and Cindy could tell he was thinking hard before he spoke, "the Paterson Black Sox really played good ball this year. They won the championship, but next year we'll beat 'em. I wish I could take that game back I lost a few weeks ago."

Nelson smiled. "Aw, man, quit beating yourself up about it. We know what areas we need to work on. Next year we'll get the title back. The Paterson Black Sox just had a great all-around year."

Gary's eyes got big. "Look at all this food," he remarked. "Wow, people will be eating for days."

"Well, that's what we want, people to buy us out," Nelson laughed. "We need new uniforms for next year and some new equipment."

"What's all on the menu?" John asked.

"You mean what we don't have on the menu?" Nelson laughed. "Got some of everything with donations, and with what came out of the Raiders' treasury. We got chicken, ribs, fish, chopped barbecue, sausage, hamburgers, hot dogs, potato salad, macaroni and cheese, collards, green beans, rice, and all kinds of cakes and pies for dessert."

"Got some peach cobbler over here, too," Howard pointed

out. "Man it looks good."

"Little girl, you want to buy some raffle tickets?" Mr. John asked Cindy. "They just a dollar a piece. And whatever the house make, the winner gets half."

"I'll probably buy some when I come back later, Mr. John. I just came to drop off the salad."

"You better get 'em now. Might not be none left for later," he said. "C'mon an' buy four or five of 'em. You can pay me when you come back."

"Now what if I take the tickets and don't come back, Mr. John?"

"Girl, I know where you live," he laughed and it made her laugh too. "Don't make me have to come get my money."

Attendance was high at the contract bid meeting for the center. It was early November 1971.

"Well, we had several bids to come in from area contractors on the building of the center," Helen explained. "The most equitable bid is from Richard Nelson Contracting. He gave us the lowest bid at $35,000. Now let us hear from our Somerset Citizens for Youth organization, which is actually under the stewardship of the Somerville Manor Civic Association."

"Helen, I think we may have some new members in the organization," Chet said. "It would be good to let everyone know who the officers are of the Somerset Citizens for Youth."

"Absolutely," Helen agreed. "Why don't we hear from the youth coordinator, Wade Bryant. Wade, could you advise representation please?"

"Yes, certainly. Mr.Thiele, President; Robert Bryant, Vice-President; Shirley Campbell, Secretary; Irene Louise, Treasurer; Stan Hobbs, Youth Representative; and myself, Wade Bryant, Youth President."

"Thank you. Ladies and gentlemen, I make a motion that we vote on the contractor for the center," Helen continued. The audience grew silent. "All those in favor of Richard Nelson Contractors for the project, please show by a vote of hands." As she looked around, Cindy saw that all hands, including hers, were raised. "Well, it appears to be unanimous by a show of hands that the Civic Association accepts Richard Nelson's bid."

———

As a small crowd sat on Helen's front porch a few weeks later talking about the center, it was easy to see that Helen was spent.

"This has been a real learning experience for me," she said. "I never realized all the steps involved in construction. The proposal, site plans, budget plans."

"That's true. Thank God we had lots of help," Cindy said. "But it's kind of disappointing that the center won't be right in Hobbstown. I thought at one time they were considering building on the land where Mr. Maja used to live." Mr. Maja had died some time ago and the building he lived in was eventually knocked down. The land had been vacant for years.

Chet spoke up. "Well, see it was sort of a compromise. The Recreation Commission, along with Bridgewater Township, provided the land on Dead Man's Lane. Although it's not in Hobbstown, per se, it's still within walking distance for the kids in Hobbstown. They already have the site over at Dead Man's Lane slotted for a baseball field, a total recreational area. So the center fits into that plan."

"Well, I'm just happy the dream is almost complete," Helen said.

"Yes, how about that?" Chet laughed. "The kids' dream of a center goes hand-in-hand with Martin Luther King's dream for a better world. They really deserve the credit 'cause they got the ball rolling. Then the way our parents banded with us to get things going, having bake sales and donating money towards the building. And so many of the white folks in the area came on board to help us with our presentation to the

Borough. It's truly amazing."

"Just think of the benefits," Cindy remarked. "I think of the center as being a home-away-from-home for the younger generations. They'll have a place to study after school with tutors. But really, it lets me know that we can do whatever we set our minds to do. That's what this project has taught me. That's what Martin Luther King's speech *I Have a Dream* is about."

On November 18, 1971, a contract was signed between the Somerset Citizens for Youth, Inc., President, and the contractor, Richard Nelson. The contract was in place to construct the Martin Luther King, Jr. Youth Center at an approximate cost of $35,000.

The caravan of cars wound its way from the Southside Avenue Park in Somerville to its destination in Newark, New Jersey. It was the last game of the 1972 season for the Raiders. Cindy and some of her friends, including Nina Van Ness and Linda Jarrett, poured out of cars to the field to support their local legends.

"Okay, let's hustle, guys," David said. He was now the manager of the Somerville Raiders. "Let's recheck the starting line-up. Rob, get in a few practice throws. Andy's already suited up at home plate. Let's go, guys. Gary, I may need you to relief-pitch today."

Gary nodded.

"Team, we know the championship is riding on today. It's do-or-die. So what are we gonna do?"

"We're gone do this," the team members shouted. High fives went all around.

Cindy was nervous for the team. Her years as a Passionette gave her a keen sense of how it felt to want a thing so bad you could taste it. That something perpetually dangled in front of you, playing hide and seek, until you obtained it or lost it altogether.

By the sixth inning the Paterson Black Sox led with a score of six to two. The Raiders were at bat in the seventh inning.

"It took Pitt to get a hit," came the anthem cheer, *"and they did it, yes they did ya'll."*

"Ball two," the umpire cried.

Pitt checked his bat. The Raiders were known for their clutch hitting. If anyone could get a hit, it would be Pitt.

"Strike two," the ump shouted amid hometown protests. As a collective moan went up from the Raiders' fans, a cheer erupted from the competitor's side. Pitt checked his bat with the next high pitch.

"Ball three," the ump thumbed.

The pitch was low but superior in speed as it seared close to the plate. *Oh, that's a strike,* Cindy said to herself as she eyed the ball. When Pitt didn't swing, she held her breath along with the crowd, waiting for the umpire's call.

"Ball four."

The bleachers detonated with screams. Pitt was on base. They laughed as the umpire endured heckling from the unhappy Black Sox crowd.

"Can you believe it?" Cindy said to Naomi. "The Raiders are leading eight to six."

Naomi laughed. "Yeah, they really came from behind didn't they? But I never doubted it. I felt from the beginning the Raiders would win the championship this year."

"Well, it's not over yet, but I hope you're right."

"Hey, it's bottom of the ninth and the Sox have one out," she said. "Look at Nova on third. I think he'll have a fit for real if they don't clinch it."

"Strike him out, Rob," Phil yelled. "He ain't got nothing."

Whiz. Rob whaled the ball to home plate. But it was low and the batter did not bite.

"Ball one," the ump shrieked.

But in rapid succession and perfect form, Rob struck out two batters in a row.

"We got the title back!" the Raiders shouted.

Phil grabbed his brother Dave in a gleeful moment. Along with the other members of the team they hoisted Dave above their shoulders.

At the annual league banquet that year, Dave accepted a trophy from the league president, Paul Scott, engraved *Manager of the Year*.

————

The center was nearly completed. Helen Tukes became the first director in 1971 as it got off the ground and was developed. On the day of the groundbreaking ceremony for the Martin Luther King Youth Center in the fall of 1972, the front lawn of the building swelled with people from Hobbstown, Bridgewater, Somerville, and surrounding areas. It was damp and the ground was muddy from the previous night's downpour. Cindy looked up at slivers of blue peeking through threatening rain clouds and pulled her raincoat close.

"What a great day this is even if it does rain." Lena seemed to read her mind. "Just think of all the hard work everyone did. And now we are opening to the public and having a groundbreaking ceremony."

It was apparent that this crowd would not budge even if it rained buckets. It was too momentous.

"Ladies and gentlemen," Millicent Fenwick declared as she stood with a stout shovel in her hands. She was a U. S. Republican representative from the New Jersey Fifth District, and hailed from Bernardsville, New Jersey. "We declare this day to be the official groundbreaking and opening of the Martin Luther King Youth Center in Bridgewater Township." With that, she dug the shovel in the earth and threw the soil over the front lawn of the center.

It's official, Cindy smiled inwardly, feeling a grand sense of contentment. *Hobbstown finally has its own youth center.*

———

Chet Williams came on board as director of the center in 1972.

It was Open House, and as Cindy toured the center she was reminded of when her family moved to 5 Monmouth Avenue. The distinct, pleasurable smell of fresh pinewood was in the air. On one of the cabinets sat the many medals that Hobbstown's youth won over the years during track and field at Calco Park. They were originally housed in Macedonia Baptist Church. However, they were moved to the center as a tribute to the winners, and as an inspiration to future generations.

The center swarmed with many folks who came to see the building and to sign their children up for programs. It was easy to see that Chet was pleased, as was everyone associated with the center's evolvement. He explained the charge of the center to eager listeners.

"First and foremost we had our first summer program with staff and child attendance this year. This fall kids came to the center each day for after-care and took part in a structured atmosphere where homework is foremost. That was one of our main goals for building the center. Also, on Friday nights we hold rap sessions and poetry readings. We're also looking for dancers. We want to get a modern dance group started. And in the near future we plan to put on African-American history plays. We're going to get the younger kids involved with arts and crafts."

"Will the center be available to rent for birthday parties and special occasions like last year?" someone asked.

"Oh, sure," Chet responded. "For a small fee, the center can be rented. There will, of course, continue to be ground rules, such as adherence to crowd capacity. And we always have some of the guys from Hobbstown volunteer as security during any event."

The Raiders had garnered their third championship in 1973. They were being honored at the annual league banquet. Paul Scott, president of the league, and David Harrison, vice-president, presented the awards.

"The Paterson Aces are the North Division Champs this year," Harrison advised in the mike. "Come on up, fellas, and receive your trophies. Congratulations." A huge round of applause accompanied them to the stage. However, the Hobbstown, Somerville crowd was already on their feet waiting for the Raiders to be announced.

Paul stepped to the mike. "And now, ladies and gentlemen, undefeated and still champions of the Montclair Garden State Baseball League South Division for the second consecutive year, the Somerville Raiders!"

Cindy thought the walls would collapse with the roar of the crowd as they clapped thunderously. The Raiders made their way to the stage.

"The league would like to congratulate the Raiders on winning their third league championship in the last four years. The players used four ingredients that add up to a championship team. Good pitching, clutch hitting, a solid defense, and togetherness. This combination is just unbeatable.

"In addition," Paul continued, "Howard Robinson earned the title of best pitcher for 1973. He had a solid 13 and 2 record for the season. As you know, Rob got his name in the league record book for pitching the first no-hitter in the league's seven-year history. But hold on, we're not finished with Rob's accomplishments for this year. He was also voted most valuable player in the south division this year. Rob is just as comfortable in the outfield as he is on the pitching mound. He won thirteen games for his team this year and had a better than .300 batting average. Congratulations on an outstanding year!

"We also congratulate Tim Brooks, batting champion for this

The Raiders
Front row, left to right: Leroy Jones, Sylvester Pitt, Gary Murdock, Andrew Murdock, III, Grover Lewis
Back row, left to right: Howard Robinson, Timothy Brooks, David Miller, Russell Murdock, Jerry Stackhouse, Philip Miller

year. Tim was a great asset to the Raiders offensive attack this season, pounding out 39 hits for a solid batting average of .469. Congratulations, Tim. He's in the 400 club in the league record book.

"Finally, we honor all of the players on the Raiders' team. You all played such a vital role in securing wins for your team. It was fantastic to see the camaraderie among your team members. You pushed each other when it counted and lifted each other's spirits at the same time. But we can't let the guys leave the podium without a word about Phil Miller. This guy had us cracking up all the time with his humor in the outfield. It's great to see a team that doesn't take itself so seriously that they can't laugh. Our hats off to the Raiders; you've done a terrific job."

Lena took the helm as director of the MLKYC in 1973. State funding came to the center that year. Her experience with fund allocation from her years of employment with Somerset Community Action Program (SCAP) proved invaluable. The center thrived under Lena's leadership over the next five years.

Cindy visited her sister at the center for lunch one day.

"Ms. Lena," little Na-na said, as she entered Lena's office, "do I have to eat all my food? I'm not very hungry."

Lena looked thoughtful. "Well, Na-na, all the children are supposed to eat everything on their plate. What did your counselor say, honey?"

"Nothing."

"Okay, let's have a talk with her." Lena took Na-na by the hand. "I'll be back in a minute, sis."

"Take your time."

Cindy used the time to walk over to the room dedicated to Leslie Murdock's memory. There was a picture of their childhood friend's beautiful face frozen in time at the age of seventeen. She smiled from the mural on the wall, and Cindy could almost hear her throaty laugh. She wondered if the children playing in the room knew the story of the young girl that smiled at them from the canvas. A sudden touch to her shoulder gave her a startle.

"I got Na-na straightened out," Lena said. "She's a finicky eater and just didn't want the liver."

"Did she eat it?"

"I gave her a break," Lena laughed. She added in a whisper, "The other kids will expect the same thing if there is something they don't like on their plate. So I'll have to make some rules surrounding that."

"I know you've been trying to get a permanent driver for the center van. Did you find one?"

She laughed and clasped her face in her hands. "Yes, Andy Murdock," she said. "A lot of our young folks from Hobbstown are working at the center. It really brought some jobs to the community."

"Yes," Cindy responded. "Hopefully, it will always be a place to service the Hobbstown community first. The center belongs to Hobbstown, and Hobbstown will always belong to the center. They are one and the same."

Epilogue

Hobbstown Today

This work endeavors to preserve and enlighten the masses of the early decades of toil and determination by Hobbstown elders and early settlers that make the town unique. They are truly the unsung heroes that brought a quality of life to the generations that followed not easily matched in today's world. It also seeks to pay homage to Hobbstown natives who were the first to break down a racial barrier, Reverend Amos, General George, and Robert Hobbs, John Proctor, Sr., James Sermons, Mary Nell Williams, and Annis Ballard Lavender.

From its earliest existence, benevolence was the culture and character of the Hobbstown community. The families were large, and the men sometimes worked two jobs to ensure their families were cared for. When a baby was born, the women came to help out with chores, or cooked a meal until the mother got back on her feet. There was no shame in borrowing a cup of sugar or milk from a neighbor. It was all part of survival and, as an adolescent, life appeared easy and unpretentious.

Significantly, and not by its own volition, Hobbstown became the forerunner to Bridgewater Township's racial conscience. In retrospect, although living in the midst of a racial divide, Hobbstown's early generations drew the best of both worlds. There was opportunity to experience stellar public schools, and an upbringing that truly echoed the old African proverb, *It takes a whole village to raise a child*. As children, we understood that the adults were the authority and, for the most part, we respected their wishes. Inherently, we knew they only had our best interest at heart.

The landscape of modern-day Hobbstown has changed a great deal to keep pace with the beautiful amenities being erected within Bridgewater, such as the Bridgewater Commons Mall. Many of the original homesteads still stand, but appear diminutive in comparison to the enormous homes being built alongside them at costs upward of $500,000. Had we understood the financial potential of the birthright left to us from our parents, undoubtedly, many of us would have held on to this inheritance.

However, as young adults, the notion was to move to the suburbs; that advancement would be easier to achieve by leaving the "country." Consequently, Somerville Manor has emerged as the dominate community, while Hobbstown struggles to maintain the spirit and ties that connected the neighborhood in leaner times. And as the town spirals upward in housing development, taking on the conventional appearance of surrounding communities, there is a profound sense of loss to those who are acquainted with the rich history of the town.

Since the 1970s, Bridgewater public schools have seen a fair share of African-American cheerleaders, football players, basketball players, etc., and extra-curricular activities are encouraged. However, as late as January 1996, students at Bridgewater-Raritan Regional High School formed the "Junior Association for the Advancement of Minorities" in an effort to improve race relations in the school. The necessity for such an organization speaks to the reality that although it has come a long way in closing the racial divide, there is still work to be done.

As I researched local libraries as far back as 10 years, little information was found relative to the development of Somerville Manor or Hobbstown. Since the Martin Luther King Youth Center was the brainchild of Hobbstown's 1950-1960s youth, attempts were also made to gather information on its inception from that institution. A brochure from the center provided documentation on how the center is run today, but it did not contain any account of the center's origins.

A fair amount of history relative to other communities within Bridgewater, such as Martinsville, Green Knoll, Branchburg, etc., is available, but very modest information on Somerville Manor or Hobbstown. Clearly, this work is not meant to present Hobbstown's entire history, for it is far too vast. However, the thought is that this account will assist in elevating Hobbstown to equal historical status in New Jersey, reminiscent to that of adjacent neighborhoods.

At least once a year in summertime, many Hobbstown descendants return for reunions if only to recapture a day of what was "the best of times, and the worst of times." To once again experience its peace and tranquility, and the air that seemed to breathe love when we were young. This story is a legacy to those who have passed on, and to the generations to follow, that Hobbstown is authentically unique.

Note for the Record: Robert Hobbs died in 1942, General George Washington Hobbs died in 1967, and Reverend Amos Hobbs died in 1970 at the age of 93.

Bibliography

Courier-News. "Remembering Vietnam." May 7, 1995.

Courier-News. "Sports." June 27, 1991.

Courier-News. "Students Try to Bridge Race Gap." January 26, 1996.

Freedman, Suzanne. *Ida B. Wells – Barnett and the Anti-Lynching Crusade,* 1994.

Jones, Gertrude. Montclair Garden State Baseball League Yearbook, 1973.

Kane, Big Daddy and Thomas Paul, Sr. *The African-American Encyclopedia.* Vol. 4, page 1000, 1993.

Kane, Joseph N. *Facts about the Presidents.* 5th ed., pages 166, 175. The H. W. Wilson Co., 1989.

Martin Luther King Youth Center. "Martin Luther King Youth Center: 25 Years of Service." Bridgewater, NJ.

Martin Luther King Youth Center. "Seeking to Make a Difference." Bridgewater, NJ.

Nelson, Richard. "Martin Luther King Youth Center: Realizing a Dream."

Nelson, Richard. The Original Contract for Martin Luther King Youth Center. Somerset Citizens for Youth, Inc. November 18, 1971.

Nelson, Richard. The Original Montclair Garden State League Roster. March 1967.

Nelson, Richard. The Original Somerville Raiders Certificate of Incorporation. March 1967.

New Jersey Pamphlet File. July 24, 1986. "Hobbstown History Project Gets Grant."

New Jersey Pamphlet File. Somerset County Planning Board.

Political Graveyard: Somerset County, NJ. Political Graveyard.com/geo/NJ/SO.html.

Robeson, Paul. www.rutgers.edu/robeson/main.html

Somerset County Archives, page 76.

Printed in the United States
48307LVS00003B/124